NO GRASS BETWEEN MY TOES

Also by Garth Gilmour:

Run to the Top (with Arthur Lydiard)
Run for Your Life (with Arthur Lydiard)
A Clean Pair of Heels (with Murray Halberg)
No Bugles, No Drums (with Peter Snell)
Run The Lydiard Way (with Arthur Lydiard)

NO GRASS BETWEEN MY TOES
The Eve Rimmer Story

EVE RIMMER
and
Garth Gilmour

Eve Rimmer
Sept. '78.

A. H. & A. W. REED
Wellington • Sydney • London

First published 1978

A.H. & A.W. REED LTD
65-67 Taranaki Street, Wellington
53 Myoora Road, Terrey Hills, Sydney 2084
11 Southampton Row, London WC1B 5HA
also
16-18 Beresford Street, Auckland
Cnr Mowbray & Thackeray Streets,
Waltham, Christchurch 2

ISBN 0 589 01090 5

Jacket design by Julius Petro
Typeset in 10/12pt Century
by A.H. & A.W. Reed Ltd., Wellington
Printed by Kyodo-Shing Loong Printing Industries Pte, Ltd., Singapore

Contents

Acknowledgments

The authors acknowledge the use of photographs from the following sources: *Otago Daily Times*, Geoffrey C. Wood Studio, *Auckland Star*, Christopher Bede Studios.

Foreword

THIS is the life story of Eve Rimmer, a household name throughout New Zealand and a wonderful personality who has never believed that achievement in any sphere of human activity is impossible. I have read many accounts of endeavours by physically disabled persons to regain confidence, self-respect, personal dignity and acceptance by the community — all of which requires a great deal of self-control and discipline — and, although I have been personally involved in some of the activities she describes, this story of Eve Rimmer has really captured me. Once I began reading it, I could not put it aside.

I first met Eve at the first New Zealand paraplegic games in Auckland in 1967, when, as a young married woman, she literally startled everyone by her achievements. The then Governor-General, Lord Porritt, who was present, remarked: "That girl is going to be a world champion" — and that is what she became. Judging by medals alone, she is one of New Zealand's sporting greats because in international sporting events overseas she has won 31 — 19 golds, nine silvers and three bronzes — in swimming, athletic field events and archery. But more recently, she competed on equal terms and with considerable success in a national able-bodied archery tournament and there is no doubt that, even if she had not suffered physical disablement, Eve would have been a New Zealand sporting representative.

This is the story of Eve the schoolgirl, Eve the self-confessed dropout at 15, Eve the adolescent passionately fond of dancing, Eve the patient, Eve the woman of many wonderful virtues but suffering many indignities and frustrations in the process of becoming accepted back in her community, Eve the housewife, Eve the mother, Eve the lover of music and Eve the sportswoman and ambassador.

Above all, it is the story of Eve the person of many parts — courageous, generous, affectionate, sensitive and a friend who resents sham, intolerance and social injustice.

vii

Her book, in collaboration with Garth Gilmour, is a revealing, frank and often humorous picture of the problems of rehabilitation. I am certain one of her reasons for writing it has been to motivate all present and future physically disabled persons.

Norris Jefferson

Chairman, New Zealand Paraplegic
and Physically Disabled Federation
Invercargill, New Zealand, 1977

Introduction

THE world has known of Eve Rimmer for only eight years. It has come to know her because in that short time she has won nineteen gold, eight silver and three bronze medals for the shot put, javelin and discus and in archery, swimming and the pentathlon in two Olympic Games, two Commonwealth Games and one International Games. And she has three world records and been awarded the British Empire Medal.

She has probably won more medals than any other athlete in the world — and that's about all most people do know of her.

But in the three years in which she and I have worked intermittently together on this book, I have discovered the other sides of Eve Rimmer. From the mixed-up teenager to today's worldly woman; through courageous, harrassed housewife, home-maker and mother to globe-trotter, prominent public speaker and favourite of the media. From peaks of happiness and achievement to lows of despair.

Thousands of words have been written about her, hundreds of photographs have been taken. Yet I don't think any of them have revealed the real Eve Rimmer.

Talking to her, listening to her, has shown me the sensitive woman behind the hard-talking, hard-living, wise-cracking Eve Rimmer veneer. I hope this book shows you that real Eve, too. Then, like me, you'll forget about the world records and the medals, because they're the lesser part of her. Like the wheelchair she lives in.

Garth Gilmour
Auckland 1976

Chapter One

Drop-out — 1952 style

LOOKING back, I guess I was a mixed up kid at 15 — maybe even an aimless one, with no objectives in life. The accident which then disabled me for the rest of my days may have saved me from a fate worse than death. Who knows — and what use would knowing be? I would still trade everything for two legs that work.

When I decided it was time I left school, I didn't know what I wanted to be or do. In those days, particularly in a small place like Edgecumbe, there wasn't much offering for a girl anyway. If you didn't want office work or school teaching, what could you do? I wasn't prepared to work in the local dairy factory office, there were few shops — and anyway they didn't appeal in the slightest as a career. Hair-dressing seemed about the best, but even that wasn't what I wanted. I was terrifically active at that age — and hair-dressing didn't appeal as being active enough.

I felt I wanted to do something out-of-doors, but this was a dairy-farming district and I wasn't greatly attracted to dairy farms. I'd been put off at an early age when I stayed on a friend's family farm with cow muck up to my eyeballs!

I wasn't particularly proud of the fact that I was leaving school so early, or my reason for leaving. But, at 15, I just hated school. I didn't mind the work; I was always reasonably bright at it. But I was emotionally mixed up and I just wanted to get out. I fought constantly at home with my older brother Ian, and I think my general unhappiness was responsible.

The problem, as I saw it then, was the school staff. I just couldn't get close to them. I was terrified of the headmaster. If I ever missed a day at school for any reason I'd be dragged up in front of him. I'd stand and shiver in the line outside his office with my little note clutched in my hand, and then I'd march in and hand it over.

"Huh," he'd grunt. "Lot of sickness in your family, isn't there?"

There was no sympathy there. It was the same with all the teachers. I could never talk to them. They never seemed to have the time.

At the time, the Bay of Plenty had none of the district schools that we have now, and Whakatane High was crowded. All the kids from all the surrounding country districts went there. We'd all pile on the buses every morning, hordes of us — including some real roughies — and every morning, somewhere on the 15-mile journey, I'd have someone feeling up my legs.

I was, in some ways, very forward and mature for my age, but there were so many things I couldn't cope with. When it came to handling a situation like high school I was, I realise now, hopelessly immature in a great many important ways. I was very lonely there and went off on my own a great deal. I was good at the subjects I liked — English and algebra — but I always felt I was a bit of a misfit. But I didn't know why and I was inclined to blame other people; I didn't fit the pattern of the place or the time. Certainly not the time. I think I was 20 years ahead of that in a lot of respects. I would probably go down well now as a teenager because these days there's much more understanding and leniency, and kids can do things and wear things that don't draw immediate criticism. These were the areas where my immaturity got me into difficulties.

Looking back I suppose I could be called sexually precocious, although this was something that was never discussed. It was frowned upon; a girl felt a criminal for even mentioning the subject. So she just shut up. My parents were from a generation that didn't recognise that kind of problem, so it didn't get sorted out. I wasn't told, for instance, anything about my period. It was just allowed to arrive. I didn't know that intercourse was connected with babies, even at 15. I was totally ignorant. I remember about the time I got a letter from a boy in Rotorua who had taken me out, and I proudly showed it to Mum. She read it and was horrified. She sat me down then and explained certain things. But it was incredible. I'd no idea that the things he wrote about had anything to do with making babies.

I was what they would today call hung-up. My school-work

didn't really suffer — at least the subjects I enjoyed didn't — but I didn't try very hard at any time with the things I didn't like. I could never understand or be bothered with geometry, for instance.

I adored expressive work like music. I would have loved to have been involved in the local operatic group and other musical events, but practices were held on week nights in Whakatane and there was just no way I could get to them. Because I was a country kid and reliant on what bus service there was, I was excluded from so much activity I would really have enjoyed. We didn't get around in cars like we do these days, and there were no athletic or social clubs around Edgecumbe that I could .get involved in. Apart from school athletics, the only other meeting I attended was the New Year's Day gymkhana at Ohope Beach.

I played basketball at school and there was a local hockey team which gave me an interest close to home in the winter. There was great competition in whatever sport I could get because of all the Maoris in the district. Our teams invariably consisted of Maoris plus me, and just about all my friends at that time were Maoris. We had this mutual interest in sport and they accepted me and didn't seem to expect anything of me, except to play the game.

There was no athletic training of any kind but, on natural ability alone, I held the school's long jump record for many years and I was quite successful as a sprinter. They didn't have middle-distance races for girls then which was a shame, because in the longest event I could run, the 110 m, I'd just be getting into my top stride when I hit the tape. I often wonder how I would have been over longer distances.

About the time I left school, dancing became my big passion. My father was always deeply involved in the Labour Party and its organisation, and was MC for the party's fund-raising dances in the district. He used to take me along, so I learned dancing at an early age. And I loved it. The head-master at primary school had believed in teaching dancing as one of the school activities, so I was already grounded in all the old routines and I joined with the locals in going to every dance we could. The high school held the occasional dance, but I didn't enjoy them. I was tall and gangling and I felt out

of things. I think it was association there with the school and
kids of my own age that I disliked. I was perfectly at ease
with people who were much older.

I suppose these were all contributing reasons why I couldn't
wait to leave school. I know I couldn't have stuck it much
longer. The mere thought of putting on my uniform, getting
on that dreadful bus and meeting all those unapproachable
teachers made me feel ill. I never actually played hookey; the
sickness, even if it began in my mind, was genuine enough to
keep me home quite a lot. Interestingly, both my younger
sisters suffered from the same problem.

My mother was disappointed that I wasn't going to go on
with school, but she knew I was strong-minded and, as a
school teacher herself, she had an unusual understanding of
kids and their problems. Pop didn't understand at all and just
grumbled.

It was a great pity — it was my school certificate year, and
I knew I was capable of passing if I tried. I was giving away a
lot of opportunities.

The headmaster was very reluctant to give my mother a
certificate to say that I had had two years of high school. He
said he felt he couldn't do it because of all the time I had
missed. The fact that I had been sick apparently didn't count
in my favour. I never worked out for myself the reasons for
this sickness, and nobody else bothered. Otherwise something
might have been done to overcome it. The general view in
those days was that kids had no right to be unhappy so they
didn't deserve any special consideration.

Anyway, my decision was made. I was leaving school. The
problem then, of course, was to find a job. Edgecumbe was
so small — it still is — that there was nothing there unless I
wanted to work in a factory office. The mere thought of that,
of sitting inside all day typing, was enough to blow my mind.
I couldn't type anyway. I was vaguely hoping for an outdoor
activity. I didn't know what, but I felt that if I could find it I
would put my whole heart and soul into it and be really happy.

The school gave me no help at all, and about the only jobs
that were offering in Whakatane were in banks, at office
desks and behind shop counters. Working in a shop was something I'd been put off already by the traditional black-frocked

slaves in Whakatane's department stores. They were always solemn and uninterested, and it didn't look as if they were ever allowed to smile.

I went into one bank to talk about a job. The atmosphere was so staid and formal that it frightened me. I practically ran back outside.

During one of the school holidays I had already tried going up to the hospital as a nurse aid. I had lasted only half a day because as soon as I got my uniform on, they stuck me in the sluice room to clean out urinals. As a come-on for a prospective nurse, it was a disaster. I sneaked out, got out of my uniform, and really did run from that one.

A part-Maori girl friend, Lelia, was searching with me, and we virtually did the rounds of the whole of Whakatane. We were interviewed for several jobs — but they were all jobs that I didn't want anyway. I may not have had the least idea what I wanted to be, but I was absolutely clear on what I didn't want to be — and that seemed to be just about everything that Whakatane was offering.

Lelia said she'd heard that there was good work available at the local pub. I knew this would be frowned on. The only girls who worked in pubs were bad girls. But she persuaded me. We went along for an interview and I was most impressed. The pay was good, there was free board and lodgings with a private bedroom (that, in a working class family with four kids, is something I'd never had) and the work offered to me was in the pantry. It was separate from the main kitchen and was something of a sole charge job, which suggested the kind of independence I think I was looking for. It included some waitressing, some food preparation (mainly salads and things) and some dishwashing, but it was all clean and the pantry was to be my own little domain, my own responsibility.

It really appealed to me, so I went home and told Mum about it. She could see I was keen, and agreed that I could try it for a while. Pop wasn't too thrilled but, as usual, he didn't say much. The locals would probably think I'd gone completely wrong; but Mum could see that the opportunities were few and far between and that, if I was going to do anything, it might as well be something I liked.

Suddenly, I was happy. I was independent, I was getting

good pay for doing something I could enjoy. I loved the activity and the hours. My vague plan at the time was to work at the pub until I was 17 when I would be old enough to enrol in a hairdressing school. But, meantime, everything was wonderful. The proprietors were very kind to me and that made the job even more pleasant. They were very mother-and-fatherly and concerned for my welfare. I immediately made a great friend of a girl, Gay, who worked there, and discovered that none of the staff was the dregs of society after all. They were all there because they wanted good jobs and good conditions, and were all helpful and friendly to me.

Nowadays, it's quite accepted that girls find good jobs in hotels — it's a great way of working yourself around the world — but then, in that little circle of so-called society, it was seen almost as a fall from grace. I suppose it was because pubs were almost exclusively a male preserve, but I saw nothing of the bars. I heard them all right, but I wasn't even allowed in that part of the hotel. Still, I often served coffee in the lounge after dinner and in there I met all kinds of nice people.

I opened a savings account and shovelled all my money into it. I saved like mad and the first thing I bought was a really good bicycle and a radio — it's still going alongside my bed despite a couple of falls out the window. But apart from a few luxuries, like nuts and chocolate, I didn't buy anything else.

We'd never had liquor in the house at home so I didn't know how to drink. My first experience of it made certain I wouldn't get the habit. One of the girls had a bottle of whisky in her room and asked if I'd like to try it. I didn't even know what whisky was; I thought it was like lemonade, so that's the way I drank it. Great gulps went down before I realised what was happening. I immediately threw up. I was sick all night and the next day, and I've never been able to face whisky, even the smell of it, since.

I was very happy at the pub. I spent all my free time at the beach or roaming in the hills at the back of Whakatane. Gay and I went to every dance that was on. On days off I biked home and, because by then I'd become a professional cleaner and housekeeper as far as I was concerned, kicked Mum out of the kitchen and cleaned it from top to bottom. Then I'd race round the lawn with the mower and spend the day doing all kinds of chores.

I was determined to buy everyone in the family really good presents that Christmas, which was why I was stashing all my money in the savings bank. Between April and November, I bought the bike, the radio and clothes for myself, and kept up the layby on an electric razor for Pop, walkie-talkie dolls for my sisters, a new automatic iron for Mum to replace the old wreck she'd used for donkey's years, and something for Ian. I forget what it was but, like the others, it was in the luxury class as far as we were concerned.

After all the basic unhappiness of high school, life was worth living. The months just streaked by. Then the happiness ended — just as suddenly as it had begun.

Chapter Two

The family I nearly left

POP had known hard times. He was a railway ganger who lived a hard and healthy life. His first wife died soon after he came back from the First World War, leaving four girls and a boy in their teens; he was in his early fifties when he met and married Mum, who was 20 years younger, and fathered another boy and three more girls.

He was 80 when he finally stopped working, and 86 when he died in 1968. He stopped smoking when he was 60, and from then on it became a sin to smoke. But apart from that I can't remember that he really changed.

He was a big man, nearly 1.83 m (6 ft) tall and about 100 kg (16 stone). It was a joke that his measurements were 44-44-44 and they didn't alter. He'd always had sparse grey hair, and he always seemed more like a grandfather than a father. It was a difference from other kids' fathers that we sometimes resented, but he showed great affection for all children, even if it was often hidden by spectacular displays of temper. He kept in close contact with his first family, and loved it when they visited him.

We, his second family, were born in various places. After he married Mum he moved from job to job before finally coming to Edgecumbe. He retired from the railways and took a new job installing the siding for the Whakatane board mills. He retired from that in 1965, and then worked until he was nearly 80 as foreman for a local timber mill.

We were lucky he was still with us. He was riding a jigger through a Main Trunk tunnel once when he heard a train coming. He jumped off and lay down against the wall. The train hit the jigger, splattering it all over the tunnel, and actually ran over a corner of the army greatcoat he was wearing. He got up and walked out and the' crew of the train, coming back to look for the body, thought they were seeing a ghost.

Another time he met an unscheduled train on a corner

8

near Taneatua. Again, he jumped off just before the train smashed the jigger to pieces. This time he had a dog with him, tied to the jigger for safety, and it went hurtling into the bushes. Eventually it reappeared, like Pop, undamaged.

Pop was always surrounded by noise. He was very noisy himself, and he didn't mind noise around him. The radio was usually blaring when he was home — preferably tuned to wrestling, football or Parliament — and he went to sleep in front of the fire at nights with the thing going full bore. He loved football, he had a passion for wrestling in the days of Lofty Blomfield and company, and he was a devoted Labour supporter. His favourite Parliamentarians were all Labour men. A photograph of Mickey Savage hung in our outside toilet; I used to sit out there gazing at him, knowing who he was because Pop spoke of him with such reverence. I didn't realise his significance until a visiting aunt remarked one day to Pop, "That's a jolly good place for him, too," and Pop erupted in fury.

His other passions were gardening, fishing and, believe it or not, cooking. He was good at all three. He and his cronies didn't fish by half-measures. They bundled several nets into a car and bounced and bumped through the bush to their fishing spot off Ohope, later bringing home enormous quantities of flounder, snapper and anything else they could catch. We didn't have a refrigerator, so it was our job to hawk the surplus round the neighbourhood.

His garden was enormous and, with a house cow, chickens and bees, he was a great provider. When he cleaned out the hives, the bees swarmed all over him. Although he insisted they didn't hurt him, we spent many evenings plucking stings from his vast hairy back.

And his cooking was superb. He specialised in pikelets en masse and sponges, and they were a delight. He was in the kitchen once when a friend walked in the back door to be met with a volley of abuse and the sight of Pop gingerly taking sponges from the oven and slamming them violently on the floor. It was a trick he learnt to make sure the cake didn't stick to its tin, but it was done with such gusto it startled the unprepared.

For all his gruffness and shows of temper, Pop was a very

soft-hearted man. He would chase us around with a stick, but he never got to the point of catching us. If he sent one of us screaming to bed, he would come in a few minutes later with a cup of tea and some pikelets as a peace offering. I hit him once. I was standing beside him in the kitchen and he blamed me for something, like dropping a cup of sugar, and, in a sudden flare of temper, turned and hit me. It wasn't a hard blow, but I was so shocked I hit him right back and fled to my bedroom. I got the treatment soon after — pikelets and tea.

He often ordered us out of the house, but he had no more intention that we should go than we had of going.

I can still remember his gentleness when he found a mouse swimming in the milk and carefully lifted it out by its tail and carried it outside to free it. It rewarded him by curling up and biting him on the thumb.

We always had a car. Mum had had one while she was single because she needed the transport to get around the King Country schools at which she taught. So in a period when it was unusual for people at our income level to own cars at all, she was used to driving anywhere. Pop drove only once. Mum was coming home by train from Auckland and Pop decided it would be nice to go down and meet her in the car. Ian had learnt the rudiments of driving by this time, so it was agreed Pop would drive to his instructions.

He managed to back the car out of the shed and across the road, but at this point he became mixed up between the accelerator and brake pedals and shot backwards into a drain. We had to get the butcher to bring his van round to drag the car out, with Pop yelling and swearing all through the operation. Then we put the car back in the garage and Pop didn't drive again.

But he continued to ride his old bike to work until his retirement, although he got so stiff with rheumatism he had great trouble getting off. He couldn't swing his leg over, so we would watch in trepidation when he came home because he had to steer carefully alongside the hedge and then fall sideways into it. If he fell heavily, we could guarantee another outburst of temper.

Waifs and strays of all ages were Pop's weakness. He was

forever bringing them home for meals, and whenever we went out for weekend picnics to the hot springs or the beach there'd be about ten of us jammed in the car. It was always Mum who set to and provided for them all, of course.

A couple of girls, about six and nine, were dumped on our doorstep by their mother while she went away for a weekend. But she didn't come back for them, so they stayed in our house, wearing our clothes and eating our food, for about a year while their vanished mother went on drawing their family benefit. They were eventually adopted out to good families because Mum couldn't go on looking after them for ever — but she was made to feel the one at fault for wanting to turn them out of the house.

But that was typical of Mum. When we had fancy dress parties in our area — and in those days there were lots of them — Mum would dress just about all the kids in the street. Very often the street won all the prizes because she took as much care with other people's kids as she did with us.

When we became old enough to think about it, we couldn't understand how Pop and Mum were attracted to each other. While Pop, although a non-drinker, had his rough side, Mum was totally refined, well-read, gentle and very practical. Her father was a remittance man who spent a lot of time away from home — you could trace his comings and goings by the widely-spaced children he conceived — and he worked for a time with Pop on the railways, which is how Pop met and married Mum. Pop, typically, defended him because he was something of a lame dog.

Mum told us once she spent so much time as a young girl knitting singlets endlessly for the whole family that she had a nervous breakdown, but we never saw any signs of tension. She never argued with Pop; she just ignored his cursing and swearing, recognising it for what it was, even though that infuriated him even more. She didn't swear, drink or smoke, but she tried to be very broad-minded about other people's habits.

She was mortified during preparations for my twenty-first birthday. Someone suggested we should make some punch, so Mum drove down to the bottle store for the ingredients and was refused service unless she bought the obligatory carton of beer to make up the two-gallon quantity. She was so embarrassed and horrified that when she got home she hid the beer under her bed. I think she was afraid Ian would get hold of it and turn into a boozer. Ailsa eventually told Ian where it was, and it was added to other beer which some of the guests smuggled in.

The twenty-first was the first time in six years I'd worn a dress. My current boy-friend gave me a Pat Boone LP, "April Love" which indicates the kind of treacle I was then indulging in. He was a Pat Boone-type singer himself and competed in the local talent quests. In Edgecumbe he was beaten by a long-haired ten-year-old who sang "Shake, Rattle and Roll" and brought the house down. The kid's name was John Rowles.

Money was never mentioned in our family. Not that we had much to talk about, but Mum mentioned once that we needed money for something and Pop said, "Look. I go out and earn a certain amount of money. I give it to you. That's it. I can't get any more and I refuse to worry about it." Mum called it a good lesson in economics: if we wanted extras, we had to scheme and skimp and save to get them. But needs never loomed large in our lives because we all rode along with Pop's "if you haven't got the money, go without" attitude, and I don't think we were any the worse for it.

As I mentioned, my brother Ian's life was wrapped up in mechanics. As soon as he'd left school and raked up enough cash he bought an old Indian motorbike, an army surplus model, and spent all his time fiddling with it. I burnt my legs quite often, hopping on the back and roaring round the block with him with the huge exhaust pipes just about red hot.

He was tinkering with it in the door of the garage one day when something ignited and the whole thing caught fire. Pop was in his garden and, for once, he was pretty quick on the draw. In most emergencies, he always seemed instinctively to do the right thing. While we were all running round looking for hoses, which would have been useless because we had only tank water, he bellowed, "Stand back," and began shovelling earth onto the Indian like a maniac. He didn't stop until he'd completely buried the bike, but the fire was out.

From the bike, which he had fun rebuilding, Ian progressed

to a little old baby Austin and bounced to and from work while he saved more money and could buy the latest Volkswagon.

He's 40 now and very much like his father — 1.93 m and about 100 kg — but with Mum's quiet nature. Although as a youngster he took little active part in sport, he's now established as one of the country's top dirt track go-kart drivers. His wife and three children all drive, too, so he's really achieved his ambition. He's foreman of the garage where he began his apprenticeship, he tinkers with and titivates go-kart engines when he and his family aren't driving them, and he also teaches mechanics at night school. He just never gets the grease out of his finger nails and it suits him fine.

Ailsa, five years younger than I, was a pretty little girl with big innocent blue eyes who has grown into the warm-hearted and devoted mother of three. She wasn't very sports-inclined, either, but she always got herself involved with the administrative side of any family activities. From school she went to work in a music shop in Whakatane, then to Te Puke to train as a maternity nurse, but at nineteen met and married Rhys McCarthy, who was carpentering at the Te Mahoe dam site. They lived for a time in Tauranga, but now have a house only a few doors along the street from us in Whakatane.

Liz, my other sister, lives half a world away in Canada. We have a lot in common and have always been the closest in the family — and what happened to me 23 years ago has unexpectedly enabled us to be even closer in recent years than we might have been. She was at boarding school for 3½ years — getting her there on a railway ganger's income was an example of how Mum tackled and surmounted economic obstacles — then went to teachers' training college and to teaching posts at Te Teko and Napier. She was home from Napier one Christmas when she met Geoff Denham, a Whakatane boy who was making a name for himself in electronics in Canada. Soon after, she decided to take a trip to Toronto. They were married and that's where they still are.

I was fortunate to belong in a family group as happy as ours. I realise now how very close we all were. We always felt free to criticise each other — and we still do to some degree — but anyone else who dared to criticise one of us ran into the massed defence of the Davies' bunch. We never accepted that anyone had the right to say about us what we could say about each other.

And that's the family I nearly left on a wet, dark night in November 1952.

Chapter Three

It was me screaming

IT was raining quite heavily and Gay and I were on our way out to a dance with two of the many travellers we got to know when they were guests at the hotel. Several took us to dances, but Johnny and Warren were our most frequent escorts. We planned to go to Otakiri, a country dance hall some kilometres from Whakatane, and we called in to Edgecumbe to see Mum first. I knew she was a bit apprehensive about me dashing around the country and I wanted to reassure her, I suppose, that our companions were all right and that I was just having a happy time, enjoying myself.

Leaving Edgecumbe, we decided we'd skip Otakiri and go back to a dance in Whakatane. Warren was driving and I was sitting beside him. I was a bit worried myself, because it was so wet and dark and Warren didn't know the roads too well.

Approaching the old Whakatane bridge, which we'd already crossed once, I warned him that the approach corner on this side was rather sharp and dangerous. He was driving a hired car, a Ford Ten or Prefect with a governor on it, so he wasn't going all that fast — he couldn't — but I still felt he was moving too fast for a corner that I knew was a bad one. But he was in a carefree mood and when I said, "Don't go round this corner too fast," he said something like, "Don't worry, I know what I'm doing."

But he did take it too fast. We went into a slide in the corner and, instead of trying to control the drift, he slammed on the brakes. The car rolled. I can remember it starting to tip, but then it's confusion. I don't really recall anything except the beginning of a horrible sensation and the noise of screaming tyres. Even now I get the horrors when I think about it. The screaming seemed to last a long time and then there seemed to be a long, long silence, broken by a terrible crashing, crunching noise and then a period of blankness.

I came round to a very quiet, dark feeling. I was lying on my back under the car, although I didn't realise it at first,

15

and I could hear very loud piercing screams. I've never been able to stand screaming females and I was shocked to realise this one was me. I had my mouth wide open and I was mindlessly screaming my head off. I shut my mouth promptly, thinking "You silly bitch."

The car was on its wheels and I was right underneath it. How I got there I'll never know. I became aware that it was very wet and there was a terrible smell of fumes. The petrol tank must have split and the petrol was pouring down on me. I was soaked with it. I was wearing a tight strapless bodice and a long full-length taffeta skirt, and I felt as if the bodice was strangling me. It was a frightening feeling; I desperately wanted to tear open the hooks at the back but I couldn't.

Somewhere above me, the back door was forced open and Johnny got out, looked under the car and found me. I discovered later that he was badly cut about the head, but at the time he was only concerned about me.

"We've got to get you out of here," he said. He could smell the petrol. "Come on, quick. Get out."

That was when I discovered I couldn't move. Naturally, the first thing I tried to do was to bring my knees up to push myself out head first. But I couldn't move my legs at all. I couldn't even feel them. I was aware now of intense, terrible pain, but I had no awareness of my legs or the lower part of my body at all. The pain didn't seem to have any particular location. It was just everywhere. I tried again to pull my legs up and push myself clear, but it was futile. My arms worked but the rest of me wouldn't move. I was helpless in that confined space.

Johnny finally grabbed me under the armpits and pulled me out. It's been argued since by various medical people that pulling me out like this added to my injury, but I maintain that it couldn't have hurt; it probably helped because Johnny was actually applying a rough form of traction. With my injury, it wouldn't have mattered because it was a multiple fracture dislocation. The damage was done already. If it had been just a crack or a small break, he could have ruptured my spinal cord by moving me like that — but my spinal cord had been crushed long before he got hold of me.

Other cars had appeared on the scene, and there was a confusion and babble of voices. Someone pulled the back seat out of his car for me to lie on until the ambulance came and someone unfastened my bodice because I was still complaining that I couldn't breathe. Every breath I took was painful and I assumed that my ribs must be broken. I didn't even think about my back. I was also taking it for granted that my legs were numb because they were broken, too.

I remember being put in the ambulance. I was still fully conscious and aware of what was going on. I was put in next to Warren. He had been concussed but he was talking. He wasn t aware of what he was saying. He kept screaming out for me. "Eve, Eve where are you? Where are you?" I tried to calm him, saying, "Look, I'm here. Don't worry . . . I'm all right."

One of the ambulancemen said, "It's not him we're worried about. It's you."

I said, "Why? I'm all right."

We were taken to Whakatane Hospital, which wasn't far from the accident scene. I learnt later that Gay had apparently suffered delayed concussion and wandered off into the night. Later, she couldn't remember anything about the night at all. She couldn't tell anyone what she did before, during or after the accident. Neither could Warren and Johnny. I could recall everything that had gone before and what happened afterwards — there was just that blank patch in the middle of the actual crash that escaped me.

I was taken straight down to the X-ray room. I was screaming again because it was agony every time they moved me, and they were turning me this way and that to get their X-rays. I was yelling at them not to touch me, and I remained conscious through it all. They finally had to put me out. They must have given me a pretty massive dose of morphine or something and kept on pumping it in because I stayed in a semi-coma from then on.

Certain things penetrated. The sister hovering over my bed and saying, "For goodness sake, don't let anyone touch you. Don't let the nurses sponge you or move you or even touch you." A nurse coming in and trying to do just that while I pleaded with her to stay away. My family all gathered at the door. I was worried about my work and I asked them what day it was.

"Sunday," someone said.

"Well," I said. "I'm supposed to be at work today. Tell them I'll be back tomorrow."

I wondered why everyone was looking a bit tearful. Even my brother was there, which surprised me because he didn't usually take any notice of me. I tried to assure them I was all right. I still had no idea of the extent of my injuries at all. No one told me that they all thought I was going to die.

I have further vague memories of various people coming and going, and I wondered several times what my brother had come for. After all, we always used to fight whenever we were together. Thinking back, it must have been a terrible shock for them all. Nobody knew anything about broken backs in those days. It was automatically assumed that anyone with a broken back or a broken neck would die. Nobody held out any hopes for me.

Chapter Four

Cook's Tour

MY first naive reaction when they told me they were shifting me to Cook Hospital in Gisborne was: "What for? I've never been to Gisborne in my life and I don't know anyone there."

Down in the men's ward, Warren kicked up such a fuss when they told him that they finally wheeled him along in his bed to see me. He was all bandaged and he'd lost some teeth. He assured me he would come to see me in Gisborne as soon as he could. He also told me Gay had been treated for delayed concussion and that Johnny was on the mend.

I was going to Gisborne because there was an orthopaedic surgeon there, but this didn't mean much to me. I didn't know what an orthopaedic surgeon was, so I kept insisting that there was no need for me to go. But I went.

A Scottish sister travelled with me. She was a lovely person. She's still in Whakatane, but she's a sub-matron now. It was an epic journey — 320 km and ten hours through the Waioeka Gorge. They were still building the road and it was rough all the way. I think they had considered flying me over from Whakatane, but the weather was even rougher than the road and it was also a question of arriving at the right time for the surgeon, Willie Park, an incredibly busy man who was being brought back from a rare South Island holiday to attend to me.

I don't remember much about the trip, but it must have been hell for the ambulance men. They had my stretcher slung from the roof to lessen the jolting, but it was still impossible to avoid all the bumps and I screamed with agony over every one we hit. It was then only three days after the accident and my bones were all bent and dislocated. By this time there was nothing much they could do except try to make it as easy for me as possible. The sister kept giving me shots to keep me out, but I remember those jolting miles through the gorge, arriving in Gisborne and being wheeled into a ward.

The worst part came when the sister said she was leaving to go back to Whakatane. "You can't do that," I cried. "I don't know anyone here."

I clung to her and pleaded with her not to leave me. Not knowing anyone was worrying me far more than what might be going to happen to me.

"Don't worry," she said. "You'll be in good hands here. I have to go back with the ambulance."

I still see her occasionally, and I've often remarked that I must have been a great booby. But she has always said kindly, "No, no, you were a very brave little lass."

As far as I can remember, they took me into theatre almost as soon as I arrived. Willie Park opened me up and shifted things round a bit and dug out bits and chips of bones — but there was nothing much more he could do. He told me afterwards that he felt very frustrated because it was too late to do anything and it upset him that I was so young and he was so helpless. I think he tried manipulation. The male nurse who was there still talks about how they threw me around trying to straighten out the shattered spine. I wasn't too unhappy about the whole thing because I didn't know what was going on. But I was unhappy, I recall, about a series of ten spinal injections which were sheer hell. And I always resisted the mask when they tried to put it on my face. If they'd let me put it on in my own time I wouldn't have fought it, but they slammed it on and that was that.

The next few weeks are fairly hazy in my memory. I was pretty sick. In addition to the spinal injuries, I had serious surface burns from the petrol which had soaked over me. They'd had to cut my clothes off me when I reached Whakatane Hospital. When Mum first came to Gisborne to visit me, she found the ward and asked someone where I was. She was directed down the ward and she walked down and found me on my stomach with my arms stretched out sideways and my head completely bald. They'd had to shave me because of the petrol burns. Mum said later it was the most traumatic experience of her life.

The police interviewed me about the accident, and I told them what I could — which wasn't very much. Oddly enough, I still couldn't remember being thrown out of the car; there had been the horrible sensation of the car rolling and then the great empty silence and the sound of the crash, but I couldn't remember an actual impact. I must have lost consciousness as I was thrown out, which was perhaps just as well. Then there was more silence

That silence is something I'll never get over. It was positively uncanny. Possibly there was the sound of a wheel still spinning or the hot engine ticking but somehow, after the dreadful noise of the roll, it seemed an absolute silence.

Apart from the pain and discomfort, I was comparatively happy in hospital. I still had no idea of the seriousness of my injuries and believed, regardless of the agony, that I would soon be up and about again — that it was only a matter of time before I got better, got up out of bed and walked away.

I was put in what they called a striker bed, a bed that revolved so that, although I was incapable of moving, I could be alternated between lying on my tummy and lying on my back. The bed was quite narrow and consisted of two sections of stretched canvas. I lay on one and the other was kept on a rack underneath. When the nurses wanted to turn me, they strapped the second half on top so that I was like the ham in the sandwich. Then they pulled levers at the ends of the bed and spun me round. Then the section I had been lying on was removed. I was still heavily drugged against the pain all this time, and whenever they revolved me I had this weird and uncomfortable sensation of the whole world turning upside down. I understand I frequently screamed blue murder.

In the upside down position, it was awkward if anyone came to talk to me. I could only see feet and legs up to about knee level and if I didn't recognise them I didn't know who the visitor was. An old lady who was in the ward told me later that she and some others would come and talk to me; they were so sorry for me because they thought I was in constant intense agony. Actually, I didn't know what I was doing most of the time, otherwise I might have controlled what was apparently pretty noisy behaviour.

The canvas I lay on had a trapdoor in it. This was essential, because I'd completely lost control of my bodily functions and had to have enemas and bowel washouts constantly. Hence the trapdoor so they could open up the bed and get at me. The trap was left unfastened one night and I slipped through it. I jack-knifed right through and hung there in a vee with my bottom actually touching the lower rack. Great treatment for an immovable spine case.

At this stage I was being fed through tubes, and was also connected to a fantastic contraption called a tidal drainage. The whole thing involved an incredible performance and there was so much junk around to keep me alive that I took up the space of three normal cubicles and was only allowed to be handled by the registered staff. Every time they revolved me, of course, they had to disconnect all the tubes and then reconnect them.

Both the bed and the tidal drainage were someone's brilliant idea, although the bed was not terribly good because I developed what it was supposed to prevent — severe pressure sores on my front, my hips and my back. These took months to heal and with other accidents and upsets like falling through the trapdoor, helped to make life fairly harrowing from time to time. Pressure sores are a constant danger to paraplegics. They and associated problems like kidney infections have been fatal as often as the original injuries.

We have no feeling in our limbs, so we don't feel discomfort like normal people when we're lying for any length of time. So we don't move ourselves. The first sign of trouble is a reddened area; then, because we lack circulation, the skin peels off and the area becomes raw and exposed to infection. Again, lack of circulation means these areas take a long time to heal, and very little is needed to inflame the problem again.

I actually lived with my pressure sores for about three years after I got out of Cook. The treatment for bed sores is vastly changed these days — and I have the proof in the scars on my backside that it's changed for the better. I got the wrong treatment. They rubbed soap into the pressure areas, washed it off, dried me and then rubbed in methylated spirits. They know now that this delayed recovery because it took off the skin surface and destroyed the natural oils. Today they sponge pressure sores lightly and rub in oil.

Willie Park was horrified by some of the things that happened, and he'd come around and blow everyone up. Things that occurred to me shouldn't have happened to anyone.

"I still wonder how I would have done over longer distances." Eve winning the 110 m at the Edgecumbe High School champs in 1951.

Below left: "I guess I was a mixed-up kid—maybe even an aimless one."

Below right: Eve at 15, shortly before that wet, dark night in November 1952. She was working at the local pub, independent for the first time.

Mum and Pop.

"For all his gruffness and shows of temper, he was a very soft-hearted man." Pop with Julie.

Looking back, I don't know how I ever survived. No matter how good the nursing was, it wasn't specialised and I was only one spinal injury in a whole ward of surgical cases.

I didn't ask any questions about my condition. I was probably told that my back was broken, but I assumed that it would heal up. Physiotherapists would come and give me exercises for my legs, and there were regular pin-pricking sessions to see what I could and couldn't feel. I was sure I was improving each time, that more feeling was coming back. I was positive I could feel my feet and wiggle my toes. Every time I was turned onto my back, I'd make the nurses lift my feet up and show them to me. I could close my eyes and swear that I was moving my toes.

In fact, I still can't feel them if you touch them. I've talked to many paraplegics, and they've all had the same experience of being able to "feel" completely useless legs. Some paraplegics actually do suffer quite severe pain; it's a permanent condition and there seems to be nothing anyone can do about it. I'm fortunate — my injury is a complete lesion, a total shattering of the spinal cord, which means I have no sensation or pain in my legs at all.

I remember counting the stitches when they took them out of my back. I could feel those. There were twenty-five of them.

At this stage, the main problem the hospital faced was that I might die not from the shock of the accident to my system or the actual broken spine, but from kidney failure. I was probably pretty close to doing just that. It was this that led them to develop that marvellous tidal drainage for me. It was a real education for everyone — patients, staff and visitors — because the hospital hadn't tried it before. I think only one person in the hospital knew exactly how it worked.

It was a collection of bottles and tubes all mounted on a large board-like apparatus in a laboratory, and it all led to an in-dwelling catheter. Its purpose was to flush my bladder at regular intervals because my kidneys were no longer having anything to do with me. The whole thing was set off by some device. Whether it was drips or some timing device, I don't know, but it was scheduled to go off regularly — and it was fascinating to watch and to listen to. Some of the nurses even brought their boyfriends round and gave me beer to help it along so they could be entertained.

When the system triggered off the flushing, fluid would go rushing round, shooting through the tubes and bottles, bubbling and swishing noisily, and then into me. The end result would flush down into a bucket under the bed. This always struck me as a bit of an anti-climax. We had some trouble with the system, and the engineers would have to come and fix it, but it must have worked well enough because I went on living.

This technique had its side-ills, of course. I don't know how much infection I had, because I was being fed pills all the time, but any in-dwelling catheter which is in place long enough invites infection. Eventually my bladder began re-acting very strongly to all this, and it would involuntarily push the catheter out and then empty itself. So after a few months they decided to leave it out and see what happened. They used a stainless steel bedpan permanently in place as a replacement, propping it up on pillows beneath the open trapdoor because we found that if they left it at floor level it sounded like the ringing of bells when I used it.

A nurse forgot to prop it up one day and I let go during the visiting period. Everyone got up and left because they thought the bell had gone for the end of visiting.

We laughed and laughed over these little incidents. The other patients were in fits at times. I suppose, being a natu-rally exuberant type, I didn't worry greatly about the mis-adventures and managed to see the funny side of most of them. And, still, I looked forward every day to going home and being able to walk again.

After about seven months on the striker bed, I was trans-ferred to an ordinary bed. This was my first real milestone — but there were a lot more to come. It gave me a fabulous feeling of freedom to be out of the striker bed and into a normal one, even though it was rubber-mattressed and fitted with fracture boards. The catheter was now dismissed for ever and my bladder ruled my life. I soon learnt to turn my-self over and the physios were now getting me up into a chair and giving me ray lamp treatment for the pressure areas, so life was beginning to look brighter. Days seemed to move faster than they had when I was prisoner of the striker bed.

All this time, Mum came all the way to Gisborne from Edgecumbe whenever she could, a long, tiring bus journey, and during the school holidays she brought Ailsa and Liz with her. And I made a lot of friends in Gisborne after all. Several youth groups would come up to see me and I met many others through being in hospital with them or getting to know other patients' visitors. But at any age, the months stuck in a hospital would drag on; at sixteen they seemed at times unendurable and endless.

I forget now exactly how I found out that I would never walk again. Willie Park probably tried to tell me several times, but I wouldn't believe it. I kept insisting that I was getting better and that I would walk again. I know now that everybody else knew I was never going to even sit up again, let alone walk, and was doomed to spend the rest of my life in bed.

That's what they thought.

Chapter Five

Up, but not away

I WAS lying on my stomach one day, doing nothing in particular. I found myself listening to a conversation in the next cubicle because it suddenly registered as important. Two women were talking about "that poor girl" who was never going to sit up again and tut-tutting about what a shame it was.

"My God," I thought, "they're talking about me."

This was something I just wouldn't accept, any more than I would accept that I was never going to walk again. Lying there, I decided to prove them wrong. That'll be the day when I surrender to spending the rest of my life in bed!

I waited until the nurses came and turned me over on my back. Then, with a lot of struggling and pushing and heaving, I got myself, for the first time, into some kind of a sitting position — and promptly fainted. Everyone came running and I was sternly told not to try that again because my back wasn't strong enough to support me.

Soon after, Willie Park came along and said quietly, "I believe you've been trying to sit up."

"Yes," I said. "I want to sit up and get going."

Mr Park said: "Well, then, perhaps it's time to make you a brace."

He sent along the guys from the splint department. They measured me up and took a cast of my back and eventually returned with a very hard plastic reinforced brace. It contained a large cut-out area because where my back was broken it stuck out in a bony prominence. They strapped me into this gadget and the physiotherapists set about gradually getting me up. I fainted many more times, but the periods of sitting upright gradually got longer. It took some weeks of five-minute periods, then ten minutes, before I could sit for any length of time without feeling faint, but I was overjoyed with every extra minute. This was real progress. Even now, I still find it very uncomfortable, because of the position of the lesion, to sit for any length of time.

They eventually got me to the stage where I could get out of bed into a wheelchair. Another milestone — although I wasn't very happy about the chair. The only people I had ever seen in wheelchairs were decrepit old people who just sat around and did nothing. I refused to associate myself with them. And the chairs in those days were so bad I didn't really want to be seen in one, because they encouraged sitting around doing nothing. They were badly designed, difficult to manoeuvre alone and quite ugly and uncomfortable. Rather like those awful bath chairs you sometimes see in English comedies. They still provide pretty terrible chairs at some airports and other places, although standards are improving because of paraplegics' demands for activity.

But, terrible as it was, the wheelchair suddenly changed my life. I began to get around so fast I eventually got to know just about everybody in the hospital and became the mail runner (or wheeler) for my ward.

Now I had the bit between my teeth. I was nagging everyone. I was determined that as soon as I could walk properly I was going home. I still had enormous incontinence problems but there was nothing they could do about that because they didn't know anything about the problem's treatment. They looked after my bowel movements by giving me regular enemas, but I had to learn to cope with incontinence myself. Part of my problem was that I had no reference points, no-one to ask and certainly no-one to tell me about the very real problems it was going to cause later.

But first, of course, I had to learn to walk.

With mobility in the chair came daily visits to the hospital gymnasium to learn how to progress from lying to sitting to standing to walking. I was fitted with callipers and the first time I was able to stand up in them I felt about ten feet tall. With these on, I tried out a variety of crutches and found I could never manage the elbow type because I always fell over backwards. But I quickly learnt to take a step or two with the full-length ones. I had to learn to fall without hurting myself too badly, a technique that involved throwing the crutches sideways and toppling forward to take my weight on my hands as I hit the floor. To fall backwards could be disastrous.

Most of the walking exercises were on parallel bars facing a full-length mirror. I used to eye the exercycle and watch with envy those patients who could use it. But have you ever tried cycling with knee-locking callipers? The swimming pool was another amenity that I would have loved, but it was denied me because of the ever-lasting problem of the pressure sores.

One of the aides, Norma Wood, looked after me during much of the physiotherapy, and she was absolutely marvellous. I guess I was a willing patient anyway. I loved the activity, loved getting into a sweat and was always keen to have just one more go. And I was determined that as soon as I was adept at standing and taking half a dozen steps it would be time for me to go home.

The whole business of learning to walk took six months. Apart from the enjoyment I got from the gymnasium work, it was slow, dragging, boring — every day the same. Even personality clashes with other patients helped to relieve the tedium. I could actually enjoy them. Depression comes easily when you're in the kind of condition I was in then and have been in ever since. It didn't ever hit me properly — though I must admit to shedding quite a few tears of total frustration — but it has got a lot of others.

Back in hospital once for a splint adjustment, I met a quadraplegic who had suffered severe neck injuries and had been told he would never walk again. He was so depressed that the physiotherapists had been forced to give him up. I tried telling him what I could do at home — I was by then nearly back to normal life — but he wouldn't believe me. He thought I was making it all up for his benefit. I couldn't convince him there was still a useful life to be led, even by a quadraplegic. He couldn't imagine how he could support his wife and family, and he was convinced he would be a burden to everyone for the rest of his life.

On my next visit to the hospital, I learnt that he had died.

I've met hundreds of quads and paras since who do all kinds of jobs and support families. But still, even with life going on, depression is a major problem.

But in those thirteen months trapped in Cook, I never allowed my mind to dwell too long on the depressing aspects. There was that much of my mother in me — I never got to the point of thinking that I would never make it out of there.

The only thing I gave up on was when they tried to make me walk in a walking frame without callipers. If you can't lock your knees or control the angle of your feet, you can't walk. And I knew it. I could move my feet, forward by swinging my upper body, but I couldn't control which direction they pointed in and my knees just folded — so I knew there was no way I was going to walk without support.

Life wasn't entirely without incident. I hadn't been long up in the wheelchair, when Gisborne experienced a violent earthquake. Not the thing to worry me normally — but at the time a girl who was in hospital with head injuries from a car accident was washing my hair and my head was jammed in a washbasin. When the shake began, she took off and left me; the walls seemed to be trying to meet each other and I was trapped in my chair behind a heavy swinging door that I had no hope of opening myself. I've never had such a frightening trapped feeling before, but I made so much noise that someone soon came and got me out of there.

I learnt to smoke in hospital. Everybody smoked there. The superintendent told me off to a standstill when he found a butt one day, but all the nurses hid behind the screens and puffed away and it seemed the thing to do.

There was other trouble. I was put out on the back verandah, but I had so many visitors in the dead of night — boys and girls who used to sneak up from town to talk to me — that I was classed a disrupting influence and moved to a side verandah which had no direct access from the road.

And the sister used to tick me off for flirting with the porters, even though they were invariably 70-odd — or seemed that age to me.

They didn't want me to leave hospital until the pressure sores had healed, but I was breaking my neck to get home for Christmas — I didn't want to spend ALL of 1953 in Cook Hospital. We had to get Willie Park's approval, but he was so busy he was always hard to find. Mum eventually cornered him in the hospital dairy and asked him when I could go home.

"I suppose," he said, "you want her home for Christmas?"

That, she said, was the general idea.

Willie was obviously reluctant, but I was by now able to take a few steps on my callipers and crutches so he finally gave the OK for me to go.

I couldn't get out of the place quickly enough. I'd been there far too long and I felt I couldn't progress any further unless I got back to some type of normal existence. I hated the institutional life with its restrictions and regulations. Despite the incidents and events which helped to make life a little more cheerful, my temperament was totally unsuited to the regimented kind of life I was forced to lead there.

I refused point blank to take a wheelchair home with me. They insisted I should take one; I insisted even harder that I wouldn't. And I didn't. Later, when I visited the clinic from time to time, they always produced a wheelchair and I always turned it down flat. Nothing, I said, would get me into one. Even when I slipped and fell over on a shiny floor, I still remained determined that I would get places by walking. Chairs were not for me.

Even now, I didn't know that I was a paraplegic. I didn't even know what the word meant, and I had still not met anyone with injuries similar to mine. What a wonderful help it would have been to have had some reference point for comparison — or just some simple knowledge of the world of the paraplegic. If I'd only known then of the tremendous scope available to paras in work, recreation and sport that others have today. But, apart from my own, there were no positive thoughts at all on my condition. The expressions and attitudes of the medical staff, visitors and my relatives were all negative — in spite of my own abounding optimism.

I wanted positive thoughts, and I wasn't getting them from anyone. I had to find out for myself that positive thinking is invaluable. It is part of basic therapy today to deal with the psychological and mental factors, but it certainly didn't seem to be then. I guess they went along with my optimism silently in the belief that one day I would find the limitations that I didn't believe then existed.

Chapter Six

Going, going . . . gong

THE day I was to leave I was out on the hospital steps with my bag packed waiting long before Mum was due. But she didn't come, she didn't come and she didn't come. I was panicking. They'd forgotten me. They'd gone home again. I was never going to get out. I didn't know our old, square Chrysler — a 1928 to 1930 model — which Mum had successfully driven through the Waioeka Gorge with all the family aboard, had broken down on the hill leading up to the hospital. They had been planning to come for me in a rental car but I had insisted I wanted to go home in our own car.

They finally got it fixed, and roared up just before I slit my throat. I practically ran down the ramp in front of the hospital and jumped in. I have never been so happy to get out of anywhere — I left in such a hurry I forgot to say goodbye to the ward sister.

When I got home a huge burden fell on Mum, but her attitude saved me from a tough and maybe even a hopeless battle. She agreed with every positive thought I had. She was a forward thinker and if I said I wanted to do something she would always say, "Why not?" and then we'd work out a way of doing it. She crossed her bridges as she came to them and, if the bridges weren't there, she built them.

We had a district nurse to treat my pressure sores and attend to my enemas, but Mum quickly learnt the techniques and took over the nurse's role completely. She handled the masses of sodden washing that I produced each day as if they were quite normal parts of everyday life. She had always been unstinting in her dedication to bringing us all up, devoting herself entirely to our amusement and education and, as far as we were concerned, never having a selfish thought. Taking me on now was a mammoth task, but she accepted it with originality and imagination.

For instance, she decided she was going to cure my presure sores with sunlight. This meant having to expose vast

31

areas of my anatomy not normally exposed in those days, even by me in my bikini. In fact, to do the job properly, I'd have to lie outside naked. So Mum organised a scrim screen and erected it on the lawn for me and, periodically, to keep me cool and the areas of the sores moist, she'd come out and throw a bucket of water over me. Only once did a caller shock herself and embarrass me by poking her nose over the screen to see what lay on the other side. Starkers, I guess I was a startling sight.

This treatment, with medications gently applied, soon began clearing the problem up, although it was three years before I could say I no longer suffered from it.

I suppose that when I left Cook nobody knew how I was going to get on. We weren't told anything or given any instructions about how I was to behave or how I was to manage to do anything. I was lucky I had a reasonably good home to go to. Equipping my bedroom was just one difficulty. I had to have a fracture bed, rubber mattresses and God knows what else in the way of essential needs. Mum had never had any nursing experience and it was marvellous how quickly, easily and resourcefully she adapted to the dressing of sore areas, the application of enemas and to coping with a major-type invalid.

That I was able to achieve so much was attributable to her encouragement — which was even more effective than a lack of discouragement. She gave me hope even with projects she knew were impossible. She was on my side when she knew I was wrong. It wasn't spoiling me. It was giving me back a life that everyone else believed was lost for ever. Hers was a rare quality. She was always happy for me, always enthusiastic about my ideas and ambitions. And she had some radical ideas herself.

She belonged to numerous charitable organisations, often getting rapped on the knuckles for trying to do things without referring them through the appropriate committee. She took the view that things wouldn't happen if she waited for the committee's approval, so she charged ahead. If she saw someone in desperate need of clothing, she didn't go to the welfare committee and put a name on a list of deserving cases. Maybe she should have; she just went ahead and got clothing to the person. She acted. In her view — and I agree — committees are often the burial grounds of the best intentions.

Pop and my brother and sisters were a great help to me when I got home. Mum was an inspiration.

She was such a good person that when, in her early sixties, she developed rheumatoid arthritis which quickly reduced her to a semi-invalid and caused her intense pain and frustration, I began to question the injustice of it all. She had always been a woman of faith, if not of a set religion, and I couldn't understand why a woman of her strong belief and immense kindness and generosity couldn't reap what she sowed. Her old age should have been so happy, but it became such misery that it was really a relief when she died. If God exists, how could he do that?

I've had the "God's will" theory thrust at me many times in reference to my own life. I've overcome my disability and been able to help many others so, according to many people, this was God's intention. I could possibly agree with that. It may well have made me a better person. It has certainly expanded my mind, changed my thinking and my values, taught me humility and compassion. But I can't equate the theory with people who have done nothing but good and then have had to suffer. Why should it have been so good in my case and so terrible in theirs? I couldn't see any good coming out of my mother's suffering — and if my recovery was God's will, then she was acting as God's instrument because she made it possible. Her illness changed her whole personality — what was the sense in changing a personality that was already perfect? There's no answer to this for me, no matter how often people quote cliches.

Mum remained a totally uncomplaining person, even when she was suffering terribly in hospital and virtually in a coma of pain. About the last thing she did was rally long enough to make a joke.

It was years after Mum and I had battled through our problems together that I learnt that new paraplegics could get extra-mural aid through hospitals. We had got virtually nothing except some help with bedding and occasional supplies of equipment from the district nurse — and even she stopped calling as soon as she saw Mum could manage.

It was Mum who devised how to get me into and out of a bath, who organized rails and suitable seating for the toilet — with callipers there was no way I could use the conventional seat without falling off.

Since I was discharged from Cook Hospital and was their patient, Whakatane wouldn't accept any responsibility for me. So the only way I could get in there was to have an accident which caused a haematoma — and there were a few of those, too, before I mastered the art of living. Otherwise I was neither a long-term patient nor an out-patient. Mind you, I certainly treated hospital as a place to keep clear of.

But even when I found out that help was available for paras who, like me, had incontinence and medication problems, I had to go through various devious channels to establish the simple fact that I had been an original patient of theirs and was entitled to their help. It turned out that any record that I had been a patient there immediately after the accident had been destroyed, so to get what I needed I had to follow an infuriating route through the channels of bureaucracy.

Happily, the hospital now goes out of its way to give help where it's needed — even to me. They now seem to appreciate that it's better to keep a patient out of hospital by providing help and support in the home than it is to keep them inside costing a fortune.

But I came to the horrifying discovery quite early in the struggle that the more independent you are, the more independent you might have to be because if you ever get to the stage where you need aid nobody will believe it.

In my first years at home, Mum and I tried all kinds of faith healing — colour therapy, laying on of hands, prayer, everything. You name it, we tried it, quite seriously. I still don't disbelieve it; it certainly seems to have helped some people — but for me the let-down of not being magically better was so depressing that in the end I decided just to live life to the full as it was, to think of the things I could do, not the things I couldn't do, to learn to live with my disability and go on from there. I couldn't go on dangling on a string of hope. I was even offered a trip to the Philippines for psychic healing, but I didn't have sufficient faith. It would have been a waste of time, money and effort. That sort of miracle is not for me.

I cannot exaggerate the problem I had with incontinence in those early days. It was a shocking handicap with no apparent answer. Apart from being an absolute bloody nuisance, it involved mountains of sodden napkins and towels. I soon learnt to recognise some warning sign that I was about to wet myself, but I was never quick enough on my callipers to get to the toilet in time. It was a real five-second countdown.

It was also a health hazard. My bed would be soaked every morning and I'd be cold every night because I was always lying in wet bedding. I had to try to keep warm all the time and avoid chills, and this was impossible at night. No doubt I got various bladder infections which we didn't know about because no one had ever explained anything. I didn't know how to identify a bladder infection, and even if I had been able to I wouldn't have known what to do about it. We decided it wasn't worth consulting a doctor every time we thought there might be some infection. We just blundered on in ignorance.

I was very often ill with all the symptoms, as we knew them, of kidney and bladder infection. I'd run a high temperature and sweat until the bed was even wetter and then I'd suddenly get so cold that the whole bed would shake with my shivering. There was nothing I could do about it. I'd try to get warm by packing myself in with hot water bottles, but the bed was still always cold with damp and the bottles raised the constant fear of all paraplegics — of being severely burned because there is no pain sensation to warn us we are being burned. Only recently, I developed a shocking burn about 30 cm long under one thigh from a hotwater bottle — I hadn't even known I was lying on it — and had to dress this constantly while I was heavily involved in fund-raising for the paraplegic movement and travelling all over the North Island.

I was very glad when electric blankets came on the market. This was one area where the Crippled Children Society helped. A field officer suggested to Mum that they would buy an over blanket because it would at least provide warmth even if I was wet.

Incontinence was an immense social problem as well. Well-meaning people would ask me out for afternoon teas and so on, but I just didn't want to go out. Full stop. I hated it. I knew what they were letting themselves and me in for. Every-time I sat on someone's couch I was terrified that I would wet it. And I usually did. This would be a bad problem for anyone; for a teenager it was excruciating. I had enough problems without adding this. And people, I found, tended not to be too understanding — although they might make a show of it — when someone soaked their best furniture.

I was sitting on one woman's couch when I got brief warning that the thing I most needed was the toilet. I could have tried to get up, but I knew I'd be too late. It was a question of sitting still and wetting the couch or struggling up and wetting the floor. So I wet the couch. The lady of the house was horrified. She made an endless fuss about it.

The fear of this happening was so embarrassing and the experience so mortifying that I was really deterred from going out socially at all. There was no set pattern by which I could regulate my life. My bladder controlled it and it followed no pattern at all.

It was years later, when I went to the spinal clinic in Christ-church and finally had an intravenous pyelogram to investigate the kidney function, that we discovered that what had been happening all these years was that the bladder was filling up but only half emptying. So I always had a reserve to wet things with, even when I thought I was completely empty. Nowdays, paraplegics are taught to completely express the bladder by external pressure, but nobody ever taught me any-thing. I don't think it was generally known then that this technique was possible. So it was a problem I had to learn to live with, and the natural reaction was to live with it alone.

But I was lucky to belong in a young family with lots of young friends of my own age coming in and out of the house all the time. My horizons slowly began to broaden out again. I was still very fond of music and into it I poured all the energy I couldn't use anywhere else. I'd never had any time before to sit down and read. Now I had all the time in the world, and I got a literary friend to make up a list of books to read and for the first time I began learning things because I wanted to learn. I read oodles of books from the Country Library Service. I even thought of going back to school, but the opportunities in Edgecumbe were non-existent and, because we got rid of the old car after I left hospital, there was no readily available transport to get to school anywhere else.

This was when I decided I badly needed a car of my own. We had very limited funds. Pop had now retired from the railways and was on superannuation, although he still worked at the timber mill. We had, as always, a good steady income, but there was never enough for luxuries — like buying cars just when we needed them.

I was getting an invalid's benefit. I gave some to Mum to help with the housekeeping, and I managed to put little bits of the balance aside. I badly wanted to learn music formally and the car was a constant ambition, so I hoarded whatever cash I could. Eventually we paid off a piano and this was a real diversion. I sat there and practised all day. I discovered that you learn very quickly when you want to. But it was so frustrating. I couldn t use the pedals and, when I wanted to play something really startling, I had either to stick a great heavy foot on a pedal and leave it there or ignore it completely. The more I learned, the more I realised I was only half-playing. I sat a few exams, but when I wanted to branch out into Tchaikovsky and Beethoven I discovered the full frustration of not being able to pedal.

So although I love classical music, playing it was beyond me — I switched to a modern course and, from then on, played by ear. I'd just plant my foot on the pedal and away I'd go.

Some Maori girls in Cook had taught me to play the ukelele, and when I got home I was presented with a brand new guitar from the boys next door as a Christmas present. And Ian, who was absolutely wonderful to me when I got home, would appear at home every now and again with a new instrument for me. He bought me a piano-accordion — that didn't need any feet — a banjo mandolin, and a banjo ukelele and I acquired an electric steel guitar. This total involvement in music helped me to meet and get along with a lot of new young people. We had tremendous musical evenings at home and I even began to go out occasionally to play for functions and dances.

Actually, my first trip out was to the local theatre. Ian, probably at least as embarrassed as I was because he was basically a very shy person, carried me in and settled me in my seat and then, of course, they played the Queen and I couldn't stand up. Everyone turned and stared at me, and I'm sure Ian was as mortified as I was.

Once, in Gisborne with a friend, Lil Ingram, the same thing happened. I got comfortably into my seat, they played the Queen — and a man in front turned and told me to stand up.

Suddenly stubborn about the situation, I said, "No, I won't."

He again told me curtly to stand and again I refused.

"Why not?" he asked angrily. He was a soldier and obviously took umbrage at anyone who insulted his Queen, as I was apparently doing.

"Because," I said, "I'm a communist."

This was my first experience of this kind of situation — although there have been plenty since — and I wasn't then capable of handling someone's intrusion into my personal affairs. I knew there were lots of reasons why people don't stand for the Queen but, in this sudden confrontation, the one I gave was the first that came into my head.

Anyway, at the intermission, the guy got up to go out, tripped over my crutches in the aisle and then saw my callipers. When he came back, he apologised and handed me a huge ice cream. By this time, although I was then sitting on a heap of wet towels and had already soaked the seat, he was feeling sorrier for himself than I was for me.

Gradually the young people I slowly got to know broke down my unwillingness to go out socially. They accepted me exactly as I was and for what I was. They knew about my disability and its attendant problems, especially the big one, but none of them worried about it so I finally thought, well, why should I? I had always realised I couldn't spend the rest of my life shut in a house; they led me to make a decision about it. So I began going out — and I found that I could have fun among people who didn't give a damn about the fact that I was disabled.

I was still fairly keenly attracted to the opposite sex and, I soon realised, it remained a vice versa attraction, so I went

Eve on the striker bed at Cook Hospital in Gisborne. Phase one of learning to live.

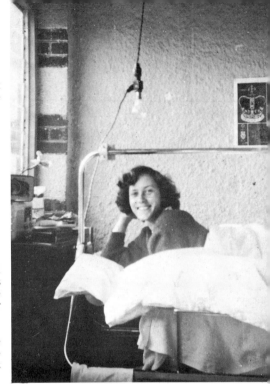

Below left: "My first real milestone . . . a fabulous feeling of freedom." Phase two: Eve moves to a proper bed.

Below right: Phase three: Eve photographed the day she first stood on callipers. "I felt about 10 feet tall."

Eve with her younger sister, Ailsa, in the mid-1950s—after the accident.

Eve and brother Ian on Lake Rotomana three years after the accident. She feels now that canoeing helped her get rid of a lot of frustrations.

through several love affairs. I'd fall like a stone and think, this is it, because I found that the boys I went out with invariably accepted me totally. This has never ceased to amaze me, because there was one constant element of me which could never be described as romantic.

Whenever I went out and wherever I went I had to be equipped with my bedpan, a handsome enamel job which was promptly nicknamed the Gong because of the resonant "Doi-i-ing" it made whenever I banged it against something, particularly against a car. And, of course, the bundle of moppers-up went along, too. Whoever took me out would have to accept this. They all seemed to accept it very well, perhaps because it was a part of me from which I could never be separated — rather like a "love me, love my dog" situation, if a trifle more intimate. They also came to accept that at frequent intervals on a car journey they would have to stop and all pile out while I performed with the Gong.

But I found that if I had the Gong constantly at my side I could get through an evening without getting wet. Without it, I was dead, socially speaking. Or a wet blanket.

It has always surprised me how unembarrassed some people can be in certain situations, even when it concerns a difficulty which most people don't like to talk about — or even think about. I remember how horrified I was when I first got to thinking about the Queen going to the toilet — you know, actually having to go and do the dreadful things that ordinary people do.

New Zealanders, particularly, seemed to become embarrassed and coy on the subject of bodily functions. They don't like to admit they have these everyday requirements. I hate to seem to be harping on the subject, but it's necessary to emphasise that with paraplegics the control or lack of control becomes the biggest problem of all. We can never dash gaily into the nearest shrubbery.

Chapter Seven

Facing outward

NOT being able to walk is actually the least of paraplegics' difficulties. It's the non-control of bodily functions that can kill you or drive you into hermit-like isolation from other people; you have to battle like hell to learn to live with it — even with modern aids.

And the attitude of people towards disability has the same inward-forcing pressure. My original reluctance to go out was kept alive because of the notice that I knew people would take of me. I knew people stared at me, and this can be a traumatic experience for anyone, particularly when you're young.

I was walking or, rather, staggering on my callipers into a Tauranga theatre once and I had to pass a whole row of women, all fairly elderly, who were sitting in the foyer. I could not only feel their eyes watching, I could hear them all tut-tutting together the way old women do. I wanted the ground to open up and swallow me. I could feel my face going red and hot, and I'm sure I walked even more clumsily.

I developed an enormous complex about how rude people were, however unintentional it might be on their part; but eventually I realised that it wasn't going to get any better. They still stare, but it no longer bothers me. About four or five years after the accident, I really did something about facing this problem head on and coming to terms with it before it beat me completely.

I decided that the next time I went out I would try something new instead of turning away and feeling embarrassed. So when I felt someone staring at me, I turned and looked him or her full in the face and either just stared back or smiled and said, "Hello, how are you?" I found at once that this immediately put the person who was staring at a disadvantage. It moved the defensive and I at once felt much better. I wasn't being deliberately vindictive; it was a matter of getting on even terms with people who couldn't help staring. It was, I guess, an aggressive defence mechanism. I've used the technique ever since. I attack rather than be attacked, and I find it works marvellously. A lot of the staring and awkwardness stems from embarrassment or uncertainty, and when it's obvious I make the first move.

Until I learnt this method, I'd go out and end up trapped in a corner because I wasn't in a wheelchair and to get up was a major effort. It was virtually out of the question for me to move around and talk to other people in a room and since people seemed reluctant to come and talk to me, because they didn't know what to say or how to treat me, I sort of vanished among the pot-plants. This standoffishness, like the staring, was because they were as embarrassed as I was.

It took me a long time to realise this and to appreciate that there had to be an equal effort on both sides. The disabled person has to meet the other person halfway. I learnt through bitter experience to appear outwardly at ease, smiling and happy, to put other people at their ease with me.

It doesn't always work. I like going to pubs to enjoy myself, and I always go in with a certain amount of gusto with the intention of putting the other patrons at their ease. But, quite often, I'm immediately asked if I'm collecting for something. People don't seem able to accept that, like them, I'm there purely to have fun. They take it for granted I'm soliciting.

And there's the other type, none to uncommon, either, who assumes I'm playing on people's sympathy by appearing in a pub in a chair. I was with a group of paras who wheeled into a tavern in Oamaru. Obviously the local populace hadn't been beseiged by a flock of wheelchairs before, and we were accosted with the accusation that we were looking for sympathy and free drinks. We were behaving like everyone else and obviously happy, but they seemed to think the wheelchairs were a come-on for a hand-out or free drinks. That's an extremely annoying situation — and it can be dangerous. I take situations like this fairly coolly now, but there are a few powerful paras among the men who don't.

I may feel anger, but I don't show it; and I certainly feel embarrassment for these hostile people. On this occasion, quite an ugly scene began to brew because some of the boys took great exception to the reactions we were getting and, even in a chair, they can handle themselves rather well. If you've ever seen paras wrestling each other in chairs you'll know what I mean. Their legs may be useless but the wheels and powerful torsos and arms make up for that.

Playing on people's sympathies is the last thing paraplegics, and especially paraplegic athletes, would think of doing. The whole point of our involvement in sport is to overcome any tendency to feel sorry for ourselves, to stimulate independence and self-reliance.

But it seems true that many people still think that because you're in a wheelchair you should behave differently, and you shouldn't be in pubs and places like that. We had another demonstration of this when a friend and I were in Christchurch and decided there was a film we wanted to see. We wheeled along to the theatre which, like so many of them, was most inaccessible. Lots of steps and stairs. But there was a doorman or manager or whatever there so we told him we'd like to get in.

He looked at us and said, "Oh, I'm not so sure about that. I've got a bad back and I can't be carting wheelchairs up and down the stairs. You people are a bit of a nuisance."

"I'm sorry about that," I said, "but I'm sure I can get some of these young long-haired louts out here, that you probably look down on, too, to help us."

So I smiled at a group and asked if any of them would mind helping us up the stairs.

"It'll be a pleasure," one of them said and they heaved us all the way to our seats. The doorman-manager type followed along, still muttering about "damned wheelchairs" and harking back to some "cheeky brute" in a chair who'd actually made a fuss about theatres and other public buildings which created architectural barriers like stairways and awkward doors.

"Who do they think they are?" he said querulously. He seemed to have quite forgotten that we belonged to the "they" so I got a bit mad.

"Yes, what a cheek," I agreed. "They should all stay home, locked up in a room and never let out. They're a damned nuisance to society and should be kept in institutions where they belong."

By this time, he was agreeing with me wholeheartedly, so I carried on. "Why don't you put a sign up outside your theatre saying 'No dogs, no Maoris, no wheelchairs'? Then we'd all know where we stood."

He was beginning to look oddly at me, so I added, "You really should, you know, if you don't want us in here."

That got rid of him and, when the film was over, we were surprised to find that the young fellows who had helped us in were waiting to help us out again. This was so unexpected that I couldn't resist saying to the doorman-manager as we left, "If you want any help in the future, you want to ask these hairy louts."

I've usually found that people, especially from the younger generations, are only to happy to help if I ask for help. I think youngsters today are better educated to the difficulties and needs of the disabled and can relate to their problems better. But it's still up to the disabled, and paraplegics in particular, to put forward their case more volubly. There are thousands of us, we are, in the main, useful citizens and we are still being obstructed by architectural barriers, even in the most modern designs of shops and offices and utility buildings.

This is why I never turn down a speaking invitation if I can get to it. It's a wonderful opportunity to show people how they can help — and I find most people are willing to learn.

When I was going through the difficult period of trying to adjust, my family was a great help. By and large, they ignored my problems as much as they could. They let me have my head and do what I wanted to do. At first, my sisters always wanted to help — putting my callipers on and running around fetching things for me — but they soon got sick of it and adopted the attitude that I could do it myself. This suited me perfectly because I knew how important it was that I should become as independent as possible as soon as I could. I didn't ever want people waiting on me hand and foot. There were, in fact, times when I resented it.

This is another danger area. It's important not to appear resentful of help when it is offered. I know many paras who will actually become quite violent when assistance is offered.

They'll say, quite angrily, "Leave me alone. I don't need your help." This isn't the way to react. If people are concerned and eager to help because they think it's needed or wanted, it's insufferably rude to reject them. The least you can do is go halfway and be pleasant about it, to express thanks for the offer but point out quite firmly that there are certain things you can and must do for yourself. If a para does get stuck in a situation he can't handle, he can always ask; but if he has developed a habit of rude rejection when he doesn't want help, he may have trouble getting it when he does want it.

My father had the right approach to my problems, perhaps to an exaggerated degree. He was, as I've said, a pretty short-tempered character, although he was generous and helpful and he was always the first to look after me when I was really sick or in need of aid. But at the same time — perhaps because I was very much like him in a lot of ways — he understood my needs without ever really discussing them with me. When I first got home, I could walk only a few steps before tottering and falling over, and being pretty tall when I stand up, I had a long way to fall, even though I'd now mastered the art of falling without damaging myself.

But there was a bit of a trap in the hallway — an alcove with curtains — and invariably I'd find myself clutching at the curtains to maintain balance and down I'd go. I'd be lying there, cursing and trying to get up, and Pop would come along and say, "What the hell are you doing down there again? Come on, get up." This was quite a spur. Mum was inclined to follow me around with her arms out ready to catch me but Pop took the view, "Oh, let her fall; she'll soon learn to get herself up." I did, because I knew he meant it for my own good and that when I needed help he'd be there. Anyway, when he abused me, I had an excuse to abuse him back and this relieved the frustrations I was experiencing in my navigation.

Learning to walk was a long struggle. It didn't help that our house had steps both back and front — I could never have used a wheelchair there. Pop put a special handrail on the steps so I could get myself in and out — I managed by hooking my crutches over one arm, grabbing the rail before I toppled over and either heaving myself up or jumping down. This took a lot of practice, a lot of perseverance and a lot of strength because, even now, I haven't got good balance on callipers alone. It's a characteristic of my particular lesion.

My sisters were helping me up the steps one night and we all fell over. We landed in a heap and, although I could have hurt myself quite seriously, we were all giggling and laughing so much that no one thought about that. The neighbours would have thought us either mad or drunk if they'd seen us.

Falls put me back into hospital twice. Usually, when I fell I hurt myself in the groin because the callipers fitted high up on my legs and the retaining bands pinched me in the groin if I fell a certain way. Twice I suffered very serious bruising but I haven't yet broken anything.

In the long term, learning to walk and negotiate an ordinary house the hard way was probably the best way I could have gone about it. I quickly learnt that I could lean up against benches and work quite comfortably standing up. It was tiring and I was always on a fine point of balance. If anyone bumped me or poked me, I fell over sideways. And I didn't always have time to grab the bench and steady myself before I hit the floor. Even today, I still tend to fall sideways if I stand too long on callipers.

Frustration was my great enemy. I think it must attack anyone suddenly confronted with disability, even a temporary one. I used to be a quick mover, but now I found my mind racing ahead of my physical ability to keep up with it. I used to be able to clean house in half an hour at the run; to suddenly find that it took that long just to begin preparing was infuriating. I had to learn to force myself to sit down and think things out before I tackled jobs, there were so many restrictions to overcome in doing the simplest of chores.

But I had to come to terms with it. It was going to be with me for the rest of my life.

Chapter Eight

More milestones

WE had always had frequent camping trips up to the lakes and these continued after my accident, leading to another milestone in my return to normal life. The whole family would go up for the Christmas school holidays, with fires and singing and bags of noise on the beach every night, and when we were older we three girls often stayed at Lake Rotoma, with friends constantly visiting us. The male variety tended to dominate, as they did at home, because Ailsa and Liz were both attractive fun-loving girls.

One night some of Ailsa's admirers arrived, thinking we were alone. They didn't know Pop had decided to spend the weekend with us. We'd settled down with Pop taking up most of the tent when the boys sneaked up and began shaking the tent and yahooing and catcalling. They scattered wildly into the night when Pop stuck his head out and bellowed as only Pop could, "What the hell are you doing?"

Another time Ailsa and I were visited by some friends when we were camped on the sandspit between the lagoon and the lake. There were always frogs leaping across the spit at night, but this night there seemed to be an unusual number of them actually getting into the tent. The boys were kept busy catching them and firing them outside again. We discovered later there were two other boys outside catching the damned things and firing them in.

Ailsa, Liz and Ian always included me in their activities, and I found that up at the beach I was totally accepted. I was appointed chief cook and bottle washer because I could slide round the floor of the tent on my backside and manage the camp oven. All I couldn't do was cart water.

I even went yachting once. It was a choppy day and the friend who owned the yacht raced out from the shore straight at a cliff face, travelling almost sideways in the strong wind. I was clinging on for dear life, terrified of slipping overboard, and Ailsa, who wasn't the greatest of swimmers, was just about as scared as I was. We were practically into the cliff before we whipped about, and I'm told our screams were hilariously funny to everyone else. It cooled me for yachting. I couldn't get over the power of the thing.

Then my brother, bless him, bought me a canoe. He saw it one day and decided on the spur of the moment that I would like it. It was wonderful. It was a light canvas job and I went mad in it. I think it helped me to get rid of all my frustrations.

I'd already discovered I could still swim. I hadn't thought I could and I would sadly sit and watch the others until one day I decided I would have to try. I borrowed someone's swimsuit and slid down to the water's edge and gradually eased my way in. I don't know what I expected to happen but, amazingly, I was suddenly afloat. I suppose I expected to sink to the bottom, but I know now that paralysed limbs are so light and relaxed they invariably float.

I was thrilled with the discovery, tried a few strokes and realised I'd won back another activity. After that, there was no holding me. I'd plough straight out from the beach — depth meant nothing to me, of course. The others would call out, "How deep is it? Can you touch the bottom?" and I'd yell back, 'How the hell do I know?" I suppose there were times when they were worried, but I didn't care. I was enjoying a wonderful new freedom.

Shortly after I got home from hospital I was sitting in the car in Whakatane waiting while Mum was shopping. Jim Edwards, a friend I'd known for several years, came by and asked me how I was doing and how I was filling in my time. I told him of the various interests I had and, although he listened carefully, he didn't say much before he walked away. But as he went down the street he saw a sewing machine in a shop window and, almost on the spur of the moment, made inquiries about its cost and whether it could be used by someone who couldn't use her legs. It had a knee control, and the shopkeeper and Jim figured if it was partly folded back it could be operated by an elbow.

The shopkeeper began to get interested then. Like most people in Whakatane, he knew about me. He told Jim that if he was thinking of buying the machine for me he'd give a good discount and contribute something towards the cost.

So Jim equipped himself with a little notebook and went around the businessmen in Whakatane, Edgecumbe, Te Teko and other areas and, by the end of the day, he had over-subscribed for the machine.

I knew nothing about all this, and was amazed a few days later when some of the Edgecumbe businessmen arrived at the house and presented the machine to me. Jim was with them and showed me the subscribers' list. The surplus donations had added a whole lot of materials and cottons. I was absolutely overwhelmed by the unexpectedness and the generosity of the gift.

It had never occurred to me to think whether I could sew; now I realised I'd have to get stuck in and learn to justify such a wonderful present. Being a strong-willed independent, I wouldn't let anyone, even Mum, teach me. I had to do it my own way. So I bought a pattern and followed the directions to the absolute letter. Even now, I still do it that way, starting from step one in the instructions, even if I've made a similar garment before. Unlike Mum, who never bothered with patterns at all, I don't ad lib except in very minor details. I reason anyway that the experts have worked out the best and easiest way to go about it, otherwise they wouldn't bother to put out the sheets.

I practised on my sisters and the rest of the family and became quite expert, to the point where I was able to take in sewing to supplement my pension. This was marvellous, because I was adding more money towards my piano and anything else I wanted. Word soon got around. The local draper, who had been one of those who presented me with the machine, sent quite a lot of people along when they wanted buttonholes made. I charged fourpence for each one. I think my current rate is 5c, although now I do work only under pressure because I find that a lot of sewing upsets my throwing arm, and there are a few more important things in my life now than sewing for a few cents. Then, however, it was all part of the great recovery to some kind of normal active and useful life.

I suffered from chronic neck pains, probably because of the angle at which I had to hold my arm to control the machine; but I was virtually sewing all day to keep myself constantly busy, so I suppose I should have expected some reactions. However, as time went by and my sisters grew and got jobs and gradually drifted away, I found I desperately needed another occupation. There's a limit to how long you can go on sewing and playing the piano and guitar, even with endless swimming and canoeing in the summer to provide a break.

Then at a party one night I met Graham Bryce, who was brilliantly clever in the radio field, and talked with him about amateur radio. I was immediately interested because he explained how it worked, how an operator could have his own transmitter and talk to people locally or even around the world. He offered to pick me up the next day and take me round some of the ham shacks in the district. I decided that if he was game, so was I. It was a fascinating day. It was a whole new world to me, and I decided then and there to become an amateur radio operator. I found I would have to sit an extensive series of examinations by a Post Office radio inspector and that this meant attending night classes which Graham conducted — it all added to the challenge.

For me he was an extremely good lecturer and teacher; he knew his subject perfectly, and he knew how to transmit his knowledge to beginners like me who had no knowledge of radio at all. Even I, knowing then only that you turned a knob to make a radio work, could see the whole concept clearly.

The new interest brought me into touch with Kel Rimmer, who was then Graham's apprentice and was just finishing a five-year apprenticeship. I had no transport to and from the lectures, so Graham sent Kel along. He had to drive sixteen kilometres from Kawerau each time and then bring me home again and we formed a close interest through this special interest. Kel took it on himself to set me special tests and supervise me in them. This suited me, because I wanted to equip myself with all the materials and knowledge I needed to build my own set. I got the soldering irons and all the necessary gear and would shut myself in my bedroom and play away for hours. I had the house resounding to the da-da-dit dit-da-da-dit of Morse code because I had to learn to send and receive twelve words a minute as part of my course.

Eventually I converted a small room under a water-tank stand into my shack. I hammered and banged away there by myself, making a bench to work on and then building shelves and other fittings I needed. Once again, I preferred to do it all myself the hard way rather than enlist someone's aid.

It was six months from the time I first heard about amateur radio before I was ready to sit my exams. I really applied myself to it and the Post Office was very co-operative. Because of the architectural barriers involved in the Post Office building where I should have sat the exams, the inspector came to my home and supervised me there. I passed the technical papers with 86 percent. When I told Kel, he didn't seem at all surprised — but I was astounded to score so well.

By this time I had built up a miniature transmitter. It had an output of only about five watts, but it worked marvellously. The night I learned I had passed, I went on the air for the first time with my new call sign, ZL1A10. I wasn't quite sure of the operation of the set even then, and I twiddled around trying to apply the theory I had learned. I nearly died when a fellow answered me from Helensville (thirty-two kilometres north of Auckland). He was wonderful; he helped me to line up my transmitter and was remarkably patient with my bumbling and nervousness. But I soon found that hams in general are like that. They love to help each other, particularly newcomers to their fascinating world.

So I spent many happy hours in that shack under the tank stand. Because I was one of the few YLs (young ladies) on the air I was never short of contacts. And my sisters often joined me, so there would be a veritable clamour of female voices from 1A10's shack.

Ham radio serves a pretty useful service to the community in times of disaster, so both Kel and I joined the Amateur Radio Emergency Corps and the local civil defence. Kel was later involved in many search operations, and even I was to become caught up in a serious near-disaster right on our own doorstep within a short time. Ham radio is a great activity for anyone, but it really brings equality for the disabled person — I know lots of blind hams who operate very successfully.

For me it was an escape into the outer world among all

kinds of people — but I still wasn't totally free.

We were by now examining various ways and means of getting a car that I could drive myself. The ham training had emphasised how frustrating it was to have to rely on other people's generosity all the time. I was twenty-one, and the lack of my own transport was a continuing curb on my total independence. I wanted to go places, but, unless there was some person available, I couldn't get to them.

The Crippled Children Society was quite prepared to pay for hand controls, but I first had to have the car — and they wouldn't help with that. One of their conditions for qualifying for a car-purchase loan was that the applicant had to be going to and from a job. I was earning quite a lot of money myself, but it was all from work I did at home and none of it qualified. There was no way we could make them change their minds.

I thought this was totally unfair. Unless I had the car first, I couldn't get out to work as long as I lived in a place as lacking in work opportunities as Edgecumbe. In the circumstances I thought I was doing very well financially, but it wasn't in the right way.

In the end, we scraped enough money together to put a deposit on a 1954 Commer van which we got through my brother's firm after he had thoroughly tested it for us. Then we had to find the hand controls, and discovered that this was done only by Leighton's Driving School in Auckland. So now I had a car, I had to get it to Auckland — and I couldn't drive myself.

But we were in luck. Kel had to go to Auckland about that time to sit some further examinations and he volunteered as the driver.

Fitting the hand controls was no problem. They were a dual control developed by a Palmerston North man called Ross, who'd devoted his life to converting cars for the disabled. He spent six months each year in New Zealand and the other half in Australia doing nothing else. I thought it was really wonderful of him because he must have helped so many people to become independent.

The mechanic who fitted the controls to the Commer demonstrated how the clutch, brake and accelerator actions worked. Then I turned to Kel and said, "OK, Kel, I've got it. Let's go."

And go we did. Kel sat there white with fear, not daring to say anything because if there was ever a first test of driving ability, that was it. I launched myself behind the wheel of my car up Auckland's main street, Queen Street, complete with hill and traffic lights, at the best possible time — rush hour on Friday late shopping night in pouring rain. We survived, but before I got really used to the controls I was stopped twice by traffic officers. I guess I was weaving over the road a little because, although I had all the controls right, I was so busy working them I sometimes forgot to steer. This did attract some attention.

I had quite a meeting with a third officer before I got out of Auckland. It began rather upsettingly when he leaned in the window and asked, "Are you drunk, or just learning to drive, or what?" At the time I was lost, I didn't have a licence — Kel was doing his best to try to teach me and I was being typically wayward, insisting on doing it my way — and when I opened my mouth to answer, I just burst into tears.

This completely wrong-footed the poor fellow. But when he saw the situation, that I was trying to master new hand controls, that I was still learning the elements of correct driving and, what was more, that I was lost, he tried to ease things by saying, "I'd suggest you go out into the country to learn."

I wailed, 'Well, I would if I knew how to get there."

He rode off then but he must have had some second thoughts because he stopped, came back to where I was sitting still sobbing and tried again.

"Look," he said, "don't worry about it. You'll be all right. Just try that hill again — it was, I recall, a very steep hill behind the zoo and I kept stalling and rolling backwards — "Now, my wife, she had terrible trouble learning to drive" . . . and on he went about his wife, trying desperately to make me feel better.

It must have helped, because I drove all the way home and within two weeks went up for my licence and got it. So that was another activity I'd got on top of and it thrilled me more than any of the others.

Again, I encountered a traffic officer who was all heart. When he got into the car to take me for the test drive, I said, 'You realise you're risking your life with me?"

"Why?" he asked. "You're no different from anyone else."

It was a terrific thing for him to say because I hadn't realised then that, of course, as a driver I really am no different. I can handle my car just as well as an any able-bodied driver; I have just as much control with my hands as he has with hands and feet. I'm a little limited at times — in giving hand signals, for instance — but nobody does that any more anyway.

Nowadays, I drive an automatic car, which is much simpler. It reduces the hand control movements from four to two, although I always found the original Ross system very easy. It was a simple downward movement for the clutch, a forward movement for the brake and either a twist grip or throttle lever for the accelerator. I now have a lever which I can work comfortably with one finger. I can set the control on the automatic to cruise at any speed I choose, which means I can give all my attention to two-handed steering.

It wasn't long after I'd found my four-wheeled freedom that Kel and I decided to get married. He promptly took over the responsibility of paying off the van and, when we married, he sold his little car and we used the money to buy a section in Edgecumbe. In those days, these were incredibly cheap in the district. Ours cost £275.

I've often wondered why we decided to stay in Edgecumbe rather than move to Whakatane. I suppose at that time I was a bit dubious about being able to manage on my own, and I felt I needed to stay near my family. Even at that stage I was still the only paraplegic I knew — I hadn't yet met another — and I didn't really know for certain how I was going to manage a house. Then, too, Kel had finished his apprenticeship, but had decided that meantime he was sick of working with radios all day so he didn't really have a job. He decided to work in the local timber yard with my father during the day and do radio repairs at night to gain extra income.

This arrangement lasted only six months, but it was highly profitable because he got so much work to do. Then he went to a fulltime job in a radio and electrical shop in Edgecumbe.

There was also the fact, I guess, that I had my roots down in Edgecumbe. I hadn't been away from the town much — I couldn't count the enforced stay in Gisborne — and even for the short period I was working in Whakatane I had homed to Edgecumbe whenever I got the chance.

Word of the impending marriage soon spread, and it got the varied reaction we had expected. Most people were glad about it, especially my friends, and both our families accepted the situation — but there was some opposition from well-meaning friends of Kel's who thought it was unfair to expect him to saddle himself with a disabled wife. This aspect didn't bother Kel in the slightest. By this time, he completely ignored my disability. He saw me as a complete person with abilities of my own rather than disabilities.

We planned a quiet wedding, preferably in the registry office, but the local vicar got to hear about it and was quite insistent that we marry in his little church just down the road from home. I didn't want an elaborate wedding gown either, because of the expense — we had better things to do with our money — but the vicar's wife disposed of that argument by offering me her own, which fitted perfectly.

So we were married in the little church on New Year's Eve. I walked the aisle on my callipers — Ailsa had diligently wound yards of white crepe round my crutches to complete my ensemble — and stood right through the ceremony, which the vicar mercifully made short. Then friends put on a small but very pleasant reception at their home and we took off in the van for the lakes, to spend our honeymoon camping. We were washed out several times, but with the help of some local deerstalkers we stuck it out.

The honeymoon had its moments right from the beginning. I was an experienced camper, but Kel wasn't — and I wasn't in a position to do much to help him. The erection of the tent was a complete mystery to him, so I sat in the van and shouted instructions as Kel wrestled with canvas, ropes, poles and his own lack of knowledge. He got things more or less assembled in order ready to put the tent up, but first had to clear and level a piece of ground for the site. He was hacking away with his tomahawk at a stubborn stump, when he

A special day in many young people's lives. Eve's 21st birthday photograph.

Below: "I walked the aisle on my callipers." Eve and Kel's mother and father, Eve and Kel, Ailsa, Ian and Mum—and the crepe-wrapped crutches.

The Rimmer four in 1962, when Wendy was four months old.

Father's day at kindy. Kel and the kids.

suddenly broke off into a wild Indian war-dance, slapping vigorously at himself.

I couldn't see what the problem was, and sat there opened-mouthed until he shouted, "Wasps!"

"Head for the water!" I yelled, and sat there helpless with laughter while Kel raced off and plunged head first into the cold lake with the wasps swarming after him.

Then, fortunately, the two deerstalkers appeared. Our friends had liberally daubed the van with slogans so there was no secret about what Kel and I were up to. They quickly assessed the situation, put the tent up expertly, got the billy boiling and settled us in for the night.

Then we all remembered it was New Year's Eve. The deer-stalkers rapidly disappeared and returned with an assortment of celebratory liquor. At their insistence I produced my piano accordion, and a real party was under way. Kel, however, is not exactly the drinking type; he over-indulged to some extent — with some encouragement — and by midnight was in no state to see the New Year in. So I was left to play "Auld Lang Syne" to two very merry fellows sitting in their Swandrys, shorts and boots.

Until our house was built, we'd arranged to stay at home with my family. We'd no idea when we made that temporary stop-gap that it was going to last for 15 months. There were endless delays in getting the house plans approved by the State Advances Corporation, which was footing the bill with its loan money. The main problem was that our solicitor hadn't told the corporation about our particular circum-stances, which would have explained to them why our home had to have certain structural differences which they ap-parently found baffling and considered unnecessary. Certainly, once we did explain to them, they got cracking, but this communication breakdown meant that a year passed before we got the house actually under way. By then, I'd given birth to Julie.

Chapter Nine

The art of gentle childbirth

I WAS shocked when I found I was pregnant.

I'd been more or less brainwashed into believing I would probably never be able to conceive even if I was capable of normal sexual relations. I had come to accept that there must be some malformation which would prevent conception. So when I realised I was pregnant, I was totally unprepared for it.

I missed a period but dismissed that as nothing significant. Then, although there were no other symptoms, I missed another. I saw my doctor and he took tests and confirmed that I was, indeed, heavy with child.

Once the shock passed, however, I was highly delighted. I suppose you could call it yet another activity achieved. And it left learning to walk and to drive for dead. I whizzed right through this pregnancy and the second one in perfect health, with none of the usual problems that most women seem to suffer. I remained active, staggering round on my callipers even in the later months. I did suffer from the occasional bout of indigestion, but that was most probably simply because I ate too much.

And once the pregnancy was confirmed I flung myself at my sewing machine and began making the inevitable layette for my daughter. Knitting, sewing and crocheting, I made piles too much of everything. With all the things that my mother and everyone else thought I should have, it was piled in heaps everywhere. It was all designed for a girl — I just knew that's what I was going to have.

I didn't get very big and, because I stayed on my callipers right through, no one knew I was pregnant unless I told them. Being fairly tall, I suppose, I could carry a child well. I think the continued use of the callipers helped because all the muscles I had left were being utilised. I think it was about seven months before people began to notice; mind you, I didn't go out much because I couldn't walk far and, when I did, I would usually be sitting — in a car or a chair — so I guess I didn't really give many people much opportunity to observe my interesting condition.

What we didn't know was how I was going to know when I was ready to have the baby. The doctor and I talked it over and he just said that I was to ring him as soon as I thought things might be happening and he would send an ambulance straight away. So I went through the usual procedures of going to the hospital and booking into the maternity annexe and being examined. A precautionary X-ray was taken in case I had to have a caesarian, but everything checked out normal and it was decided a surgical delivery wouldn't be necessary.

Then I went home to wait — and add to the piles of baby clothing. I did get pretty uncomfortable at the end, but the night before the baby was actually scheduled to arrive Kel and I went visiting friends. We had quite a long drive to their house and then I had to climb some steps to get inside. We stayed quite late and I had to walk out again and make the long drive home. When we finally got to bed that night, I was in real discomfort. I didn't know which way to lie and I began to wonder if things were happening. The contractions seemed to be there but there was no associated pain. I didn't really know what was happening until the waters broke and flooded the bed. Even then I wasn't absolutely sure because I flooded the bed every night anyway.

I thought, "Oh, God, something must be happening now," but it was still somewhat confusing. Women become incontinent to some degree in the later stages of pregnancy, so I was doubly bad. But, eventually, I thought, "I can't really have done that much in the bed," so I called to Kel and suggested that he'd better call the doctor. Kel hurtled out of bed and, since he can't see too well at the best of times, did all the wrong things fathers-to-be are supposed to do, putting his trousers on back to front and tripping over things in his haste to reach the telephone.

By the time the ambulance screamed around, I think things were well on the way. I remember my hands were shaking like leaves in the wind, and it took me the whole trip into the hospital to get a cigarette lit to calm myself down. I got there only just in time and they rushed me straight to the delivery room. Here a young nurse tried to treat me like a normal person by attempting to do a prep on me. I tried explaining that she couldn't do that. I was quoting the law, you know, that any action brings reaction and pointing out that if she gave me an enema everything would work and cause total disaster because I had no control over anything. She wouldn't listen, of course, and went right ahead.

Fortunately the baby's head suddenly began appearing and the nurse dropped everything. Then the doctor arrived and everything was brought under control. It was fantastic. I was more or less able to watch everything. I was trying to sit up the whole time, which was a little confusing because they weren't sure how to distribute me on the table. I had one leg up around the doctor's neck, the other held inelegantly by the sister.

· I didn't have to do much to help the birth — I couldn't anyway — because Julie was virtually delivering herself. When she finally appeared in my line of vision, I couldn't get over the size of her. She looked huge. I couldn't understand where she all came from. In fact, she was quite small — about 2.7 kg. I was thrilled and so was the whole theatre staff. I watched them tying the cord and cleaning her up, and then they gave her to me, because I was feeling quite marvellous. There was absolutely no exhaustion or pain.

Once I got hold of her, I wanted to leave the delivery room at once.

"Oh, no" the doctor reminded me. "We're not finished yet. We've got to wait until the placenta comes away."

Hell, I'd completely forgotten about that. So I had to lie back and relax again. The afterbirth was interesting in itself because the whole business of birth was totally new to me, and I was enjoying what was virtually a grandstand seat for the whole process. The doctor was as happy as Larry, remarking on the quality of the placenta and how efficiently I was disposing of it. I thought it was rather a mess.

Kel meantime had been dancing about in the corridor waiting — he suffered far more than I did because he desperately wanted to go the toilet and he couldn't find one and there didn't seem to be anybody about to tell him where to go. But he was able, like me, to see the baby straight away — and then he got some directions and rushed off to solve his other problem.

I didn't know much about babies then — only what little I'd been told and what little I'd read. My instinct immediately was to put the baby to the breast, but they carted her off. I was furious. And the result was that I had great trouble with my breasts for the first few days; among the things that I didn't know is that the first of a mother's milk is colostrum and unless this is expressed or given to the baby it clogs the canals and ducts and inhibits the normal milk flow. Apparently the nurses didn't know anything about it, either. I was appalled by their lack of basic knowledge.

I remember that, before I was raced into the delivery room, I was asked as part of the routine questioning if I was going to breast feed.

"Of course," I replied, "doesn't everybody?"

"Oh, no," the nurse said, "you don't have to if you don't want to."

I had assumed this was something all mothers did, and I was staggered at the suggestion that it wasn't really necessary. Possibly I'd been influenced by Pop's attitude; whenever he saw a mother who wasn't breast feeding a small baby, he would demand, "What's wrong with you woman? Why aren't you feeding your baby yourself? I swung off my mother until I was four years old." And, of course, Mum breast fed all of us and apparently enjoyed it. And we were all fine healthy kids.

I asked the nurse what would happen if I said "No," and she said I would be injected to stop the milk. I was even more aghast at this, because to have to dry the supply up seemed even more unnatural.

Anyway, they wouldn't let me have the baby straight away and the colostrum build-up gave me several days of real trouble with hard swollen breasts. When they finally brought Julie to me for feeding, they handed me water, explaining that since I wasn't giving milk properly she had to have something. Fortunately Julie was a strong sucker, and between us everything began functioning properly. By the time I went home she was putting on weight and recovering what she'd lost during the first few days.

I had gallons of milk and this added to my annoyance that I hadn't known enough — nor had anyone else — to draw off the colostrum at the start. I studied the subject more closely after this experience and realised all the more how utterly stupid the whole procedure had been. We should really follow nature when we can; I know that if I'd had the baby at home, she would have been put on the breast immediately.

Quite apart from the value to the baby, breast feeding was a tremendous feeling. People who don't breast feed their babies when they could don't know the experience they're missing. It's just wonderful to have your baby nestled there, sucking contentedly with its little hands clinging to you. This is a time when you feel a oneness with your baby; it's a time when she's yours and yours alone. I was somewhat of a jealous mother at any time. I was very strong and I wouldn't let anyone else handle Julie. I didn't want anyone to even look at her. She was mine. I had the same intense feeling when I had Wendy, although I then had to share her with Julie. Julie was two years old by then, and she was constantly wanting to help and get in the act. Even with the breast feeding. She so wanted to be involved that more than once I had Wendy on one breast and Julie on the other. I had fed her so long that way that I guess she still considered it her domain.

I took Julie home from the hospital to Mum's place. Visitors used to take Mum aside and ask, "I suppose, of course, that you look after the baby?"

Mum would answer, "I'm lucky if I can even get to look at her, let alone look after her."

But most people still took it for granted that I would be incapable of managing. Mum's house certainly wasn't too convenient for me, but I was determined to manage. I used to sit on the bathroom floor and lean over and bathe her in the big bath with all the towels and nappies and things spread around me where I could get at them. In fact the bathroom floor was my operational headquarters for most activities with Julie, because there she was safe. A baby can't fall off the floor.

It was impossible for me to carry her, of course, and extremely difficult to push her in the pram. I'd take two steps and push one; take two steps and push one. It was slow and laborious but I got there — on my own. In one sense, living at home had its advantages because the others could help to speed up the baby-minding process to some extent. Pop was wonderful; he loved babies and children in his own gruff way. And she learnt to sleep through anything because the house was always filled with noise. There'd be records playing and radios blaring, but Julie slumbered happily through it all.

In planning our house, we paid particular attention to the problems of handling a baby. We concentrated on the bedroom because I decided it would be easiest for me to handle her from the bed. So we installed a hand basin with hot and cold water by the bed as part of a window seat running right along the wall so that I could place things on it, handle the baby and do virtually everything, including look after myself, virtually from the one comfortable spot.

When we did finally shift into the house and Wendy was born, she was much easier to look after. I kept her in the bedroom with me and when she woke up I could pick her straight from the pram and bathe, feed and change her without getting up. I developed a great technique for scooping her out of the pram with one hand because if I tried to lean over and use both hands I'd lose balance and take a header onto the floor. I used to hang on with one hand and use the other to wrap a nappy round her and lift her like the traditional stork.

There was nothing I couldn't do with the babies except take them for walks, but there were always plenty of volunteers around for that. I could take them out in the car, of course, although this was quite an operation if I was on my own. We still had the Commer then, with a car seat for Julie and a carrycot for Wendy. It sounds simple enough, but it was quite a circus getting them and myself into the car without any assistance.

As they grew older, I found the stroller pram — the type in which the baby sits with her legs through openings in the canvas seat facing the pusher — was ideal because I could wheel that to the car and use my one-handed scoop trick to pick them out and place them in the carrycot or the car seat. Years of standing and walking on crutches, fortunately, had made me much stronger than most women in the arms and shoulders.

In fact I had to be careful about my strength. When Wendy got big enough I began bathing her in the big bath. I'd run the bathwater and then sit on the floor so that I could use both arms to lift her in and wash her. Then I'd fish her out and roll her around on towels on the floor to dry her. I noticed several times that I left bruises on her because I'd held her too firmly without realising it.

This routine went on with both of them until they were old enough to be left in the bath unsupervised — and I've always believed kids have to be pretty old before you can take that kind of risk.

To get everything done involved a very strict routine because every chore was so time-consuming. With two children, my days were very full.

But I'm skipping the biggest complication of all. It hit us just about the time the builders began on our house. It was the most incredible piece of bad luck — reducing us to one pair of arms and one pair of legs right at one of the most hectic periods of our lives.

Chapter Ten

Half-man, half-woman

KEL came home from work one day feeling very ill. He vomited without stopping for three days and suffered a continual and dreadful headache. The doctor at first diagnosed it as gastric flu but Kel was convinced it was polio. I wouldn't believe that, of course, but this was 1961, just before the general introduction of the Salk anti-poliomyelitis vaccine. It was available; all babies had it and I think children could get it free and adults could be injected if they went to their doctors and paid for it. Not many bothered, naturally. I suppose we all worked on the principle, "It'll never happen to us."

Anyway, there were no signs of paralysis when the doctor first examined Kel, but after three days, when he was much worse, he came back and went all over Kel most thoroughly with his little hammer. Kel had now weakened considerably and could no longer use his arms. The doctor agreed this time that it possibly was polio and Kel was taken by ambulance to Whakatane Hospital. Here the diagnosis was confirmed and Kel became one of the last cases in New Zealand.

It was already definite by the time I got to the hospital, but they still had no idea how bad it might get because there was no way of stopping it once it started. It was still obviously getting worse so it was decided to move him immediately to the respiratory unit in the Auckland Hospital. Kel was in isolation and I had to watch from a distance as he thrashed about on the bed. They wouldn't let me near him which I thought was ridiculous because I'd been thoroughly exposed to the virus over the previous few days and I couldn't see that it would make any difference now.

Then they asked me if I'd like to travel to Auckland in the ambulance with Kel but I couldn't see any point in that, either. I would have been more trouble to look after than Kel. I told them if they could assure me he wasn't going to die I'd prefer to follow up in my car with Julie and my mother so that I could spend more time in Auckland with him.

As an added complication, the Commer van was stripped down at the time because Kel had been grinding the valves, so I had to get it slapped back together in a hell of a hurry. Then away we went to Auckland.

The word about Kel soon got around the ham radio network. I don't remember now whether I went on the air and told someone or whether someone else around the district did it for me, but I immediately got offers of help from hams in Auckland. All sorts of people came forward and they were absolutely marvellous in putting us up in their homes and looking after us and taking us to the hospital. Kel by this time was almost helpless. He couldn't do anything with his arms at all. But he only spent one night in the iron lung, because the polio stopped spreading when it reached chest level; he could still breathe by himself, even though it was difficult. He wás receiving excellent treatment. Conditions in the isolation block were hopelessly crowded, but they knew exactly what they were doing.

Getting to see him was quite a performance. I had to take Mum up to the hospital with me to look after Julie, who was then only thirteen months old — I wasn't going to be separated from them both at the same time — and then she'd take Julie off to look at the ducks in the Domain while I donned a gown and mask and was taken in to Kel. But I couldn't stay in Auckland indefinitely, and when it became obvious that Kel wasn't going to get any worse I decided I would have to return home.

Then, wonderfully, the hams in Auckland played their trump card. From somewhere they got hold of an old ZC1 transmitting set and arranged to have it installed by Kel's bed. This meant that when I got home to Edgecumbe, I could still talk to him. When the reception was bad, and it often was, the hams along the route would pick up our conversation and relay it along for us. Hams love listening in, and they were completely marvellous in this situation. Kel always got the message from me and the answer back to me somehow.

At the same time, there were other hams in hospitals throughout New Zealand and when Kel's case was publicised in the newspapers — we made quite a few headlines, of course, because not many paraplegic wives wind up with paralysed husbands — many of them also had sets installed until finally the country had a whole hospital net operating at certain times of the day. It was a wonderful thing, especially for people like Kel who couldn't do anything except lie helplessly in bed.

Kel was finally moved back to Whakatane Hospital and I was then able to take Julie in to see him several times a week, which nearly gave him heart failure as well because she was an active little thing and she terrified him when she hopped on the bed. He knew he couldn't catch her if she fell. But she never did.

Our house was by now finally being built, and it was my job to go round there and supervise proceedings and report back to Kel. He was highly frustrated because we had designed so much of the house ourselves and he wanted to be on the spot. Every time I reported progress, he would give me a great list of instructions to take back so that I could check exactly on what the builders were doing.

Six months of this dragged by, and the doctor finally told Kel he could go home if he could walk from the hospital to his mother's place. It was a tall challenge because it was about three kilometres, but Kel was so determined that he made it, tottering along with his useless arms hanging like a zombie's. At first, he came home only for weekends; then, he left the hospital and attended physiotherapy as an out patient.

And then, to cap it, I discovered I was pregnant with Wendy. The Rimmers' life is never dull. All I could say to Kel when it was confirmed was, "Goodness gracious, I'm going to have another baby."

Kel had no power in his hands or fingers. He couldn't carve meat or cut bread or do up buttons because there was no grip. And he couldn't raise his arms up at all. He endured months of patient exercise before he could lift them to waist level. He exercised by swaying his body and heaving his arms up to a mark on the door. Dogged perseverance finally got him to the stage of reaching up to shoulder level and he then added an object weighing about a couple of kilograms to add resistance. At first, he couldn't lift even that little weight two or three times without tiring; in fact, he cheated a bit at first by using a piece of elastic instead of cord on his weights.

Even eating was a problem in those early days — he had to have his face practically down in his plate because he couldn't lift anything up to it.

So, a half-man and a half-woman, with a baby and another on the way, we moved into our new house. We'd always intended to do a great deal of the finishing ourselves and we hadn't changed our minds, even though we'd no idea now how we were going to manage, so that was how the builders left it for us. It became a battle of trial, error and frustration, but we found that with a bit of forethought and planning we could do most jobs together. I did all the arm work and Kel did the leg work and when there were tasks that needed both arms and legs we combined forces. For instance, to hang our curtains, Kel would lock his arms round me — he could lift them and lock them at waist level — and then brace himself while I reached up. I can remember even being in the bath once, putting curtains on the high shelves above it. I can't recall now how on earth I got there. But it worked. Kel quite enjoyed acting as my legs although he nearly collapsed us completely with some of his cracks about the positions we got into.

Since then Kel has never stopped working at regaining the use of his arms. Some of the muscles will never work again, but he can now lift much higher than waist level. His thumbs were his biggest problem. They just wouldn't operate, although Willie Park, who had looked after me in Cook Hospital, kept him at them. Then Mr Park moved to Auckland, and Coates Milson of Tauranga took his place. He used to tell Kel that as far as he was concerned Kel had reverted to an ape because the main difference between man and ape is the muscle which controls the particular movements of thumb. You know how a monkey or an ape will always grab a banana in its palm and curl its fingers round it; it can't use its thumb the way humans do to pick things up. That's just the way Kel was.

But at last he produced a new idea by announcing that he would operate on Kel to replace the useless tendon that prevented him from having normal thumbs. He told us vaguely what he intended to do, but he didn't tell us that he had never done an operation like this before. It was an awkward and not entirely painless operation because he grafted a tendon into the thumb from the inside of Kel's wrist. He was delighted with the result of the operation on the first hand and even called Kel into the hospital one day so that he could demonstrate to a seminar how Kel could wiggle his thumb. But Kel refused to have the other thumb transplant and worked to get it back into action naturally. It took a lot longer, but it finally made it.

The recovery of thumb power was important to us because it enabled Kel to go back to his job as a radio and electrical repairman. The owner of the shop, Keith Heydon, a builder, had often gone with me to see Kel when he was in hospital and he kept the job open for him until he was ready to get back into it. Keith was a great sportsman and boss and a wonderful friend.

He gave us a house-warming when we moved in. We expected it to be a little embarrassing because, owing to the setback, we had no chairs, no furniture, no money, no anything, apart from a few Woolworth's knives and forks, a bed each and the ton of stuff that Julie seemed to have acquired. She had more than Kel and I together. We really felt we couldn't afford a house-warming, because we didn't even have a carpet for guests to sit on, so it was a surprise when Keith and his friends turned up.

The first thing he said when he walked in the door was "By God, Rimmer, you're a beaut. You get us round here and you've got nothing to sit on." Then they all trooped out again and came back with four brand-new chairs for us as a house-warming present.

Kel began working for an hour or so each day in the shop, and gradually built up until he was working fulltime again. This was his big milestone because there had been a time when the occupational therapist in Auckland told him he would never be able to work at his job again and should think about finding something else to do. I suppose it was well-meant advice, but it was shattering for Kel because he'd worked hard and was exceptionally well-qualified in his trade. I was absolutely livid at the time, refusing to believe that he was going to waste all his time and experience. He'd always been mad on radio — it was his life's work, not the sort of thing you could just throw away.

These first weeks in the new home were incredibly hectic. Even getting a clothesline rigged up so that I could use it was a major operation. Obviously I couldn't use any kind of standard line, but Kel finally devised a continuous line which revolved round a bicycle wheel at either end. I could operate one wheel from my callipers — and later from a sitting position — without having to move from the bench where I stacked the washing. I just pegged the clothes up and wound them out over the lawn as I went.

I also discovered that although I'd thought I'd been managing well on my own before, other people had been doing things for me that I'd never really thought about. Now I was really on my own, because even Kel couldn't do a lot of these chores. I found that life was a lot more complicated and fully occupied than I'd imagined. And with another baby on the way, too.

I had to learn to handle the house by myself totally — all the meals, the washing and cleaning, looking after Julie, preparing for Wendy. There always seemed to be a million chores, every one taking me longer than it would take anyone else. There was one good thing — it didn't give me time to sit down and feel sorry for myself.

With Pop's help, Kel dug a garden for vegetables and, very painstakingly, built a terrace and a workshop. Kel is inclined to be quiet and shy, but he's damned stubborn and what he achieved was far more of a feat than you could imagine. He could hold a hammer only by using two hands and he could barely lift it high enough to get any force into hitting a nail. It took about half an hour to hammer one in. He had so little strength, but he had an endless supply of dogged guts, which was just as well because he was a perfectionist in every job he undertook.

It was painful to watch him filling in the terrace. He couldn't possibly wheel a barrowful of earth, even if he could have filled it or lifted it. He could hardly hold a shovel, but he stuck at it, little by little, until he'd filled the whole terrace and concreted it, built a complete workshop for the ham radio equipment - and put up the aerials.

Our section backed onto a bowling green. Down by the boundary fence Kel, with Pop's help, established a reasonable sort of vegetable garden. He would work away at tilling and weeding it, struggling with a shovel he couldn't hang on to, until he would finally drop in his tracks from exhaustion and lie comatose among the cabbages until he recovered enough to carry on.

On bowling days, the bowlers would lean interestedly over the fence. Of course when they saw Kel sprawled on the ground they would assail him with jocularly rude remarks — since they weren't aware of the disability he was operating against — about going to sleep on the job and living the easy life. All Kel could do about the banter was go on lying there and mumble something about the garden being a great place for sunbathing. There was no way he was going to explain to them exactly why he was lying down.

Kel had a stubborn pride and determination about his problem. Once he was carrying a load of timber across a road in Whakatane and he was about halfway across when he realised he was going to drop the lot. Once a polio person's fingers begin to unwind, there's just nothing he can do to stop it. So he dropped the lot. And then he patiently had to pick the timber up piece by piece and move it all to the roadside. The startled looks on the faces of the passersby told him what an odd person they thought he was.

I could appreciate Kel's determination to get there by himself. With paras, it's pride that suffers most; we are constantly running into situations that destroy pride and independence and we don't take them lightly. It's all a matter of not wanting to feel foolish. I know a lot of us do things we shouldn't do — or don't do things we should do — to avoid this feeling.

For instance Kel can't see in the dark — in theatres he blunders around until people start yelling at him to sit down, and then he's quite liable to sit on the floor or blunder right out again — but he'll go to extraordinary lengths not to have to admit it. In daytime his vision doesn't let him see people at a distance. A car once drew in beside him with the back door open. Kel thought it was an announcer from Radio Whakatane offering him a lift so he jumped in. He was rather startled when someone else climbed in after him, and even more startled to discover he was in a car full of total strangers.

He was quite cool about it, though. "You can drop me at the radio station, thanks," he said. Without a word, the driver delivered him to Radio Whakatane. We often wonder what he and his companions were thinking.

Little Wendy arrived while all this was going on. This time I was so positive she was going to be a boy that we'd already named her Danny after my grandfather — Mark Daniel. Come to think of it, I suppose I could have compromised when we discovered our mistake in judgment by calling her Danielle, but when I first saw her she looked so small and cute, so like a Wendy, that she became Wendy immediately.

It's hard now to remember that I was carrying her all through this unbelievable settling-in period. I know I'd try to mop the floor on my crutches and fall over many times and think to myself, "Any minute, now, and I'm going to have a miscarriage," then I'd get up and keep going. And Wendy arrived right on schedule, twice as fast and twice as easily as Julie. I had a wonderful time, annoying everybody once again by sitting up and trying to watch everything. She was small, only 2.49 kg, but she was a wriggly little thing from the start and she thrived. Once again, I had milk to spare and this time breast feeding began right away.

Kel brought Julie in when he came to take us home. He'd told Julie they were going to get me and a little baby. "Oh," Julie said, "I don't want a baby. I want to go and see Nanna's cat!" But once we got home, she very quickly developed an interest in Wendy, as if she was a cat or a dog. In fact I found it a bit of a strain at times because she was then a very forward two-year-old, talking all the time and desperately wanting to help. Things didn't really get easier until she began going to the kindergarten round the corner and gave me some hours of peace for at least five days a week.

I've always been perfectly happy that both our children are girls. They're both sports mad and pretty resilient. They like feminine things, but they're always involved in a mass of activities — Wendy's latest was a horse and looking after the broken arm she got when she fell off it — and as little kids they played with trucks and things rather than dolls. As

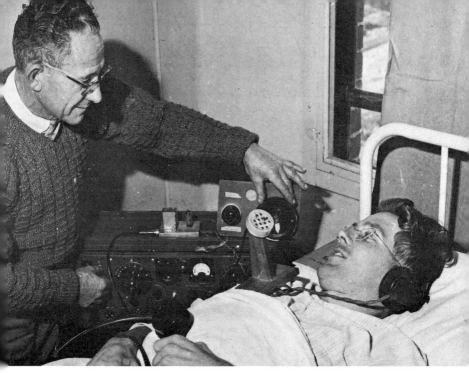

Rimmer in Auckland ~~hosp~~ital in 1961 after his seri- ~~ous~~ polio attack. An Auck- ~~land~~ radio ham is installing ~~the~~ equipment that enabled ~~him~~ to talk to Eve in Edge- ~~cum~~be.

~~I~~t was quite a send-off. Eve ~~a~~t Whakatane Airport, about ~~t~~o depart on her first overseas ~~s~~ports trip—to Israel, 1968.

Above: Triumph for Eve in her first international competition. A gold in the javelin, a silver in the shot and a bronze in the discus at the 1968 Paraplegic Olympic Games in Israel.

Right: "I was ready to chuck everything and join the Ironside gang—just to go on enjoying the pleasure of his company." Eve with "Ironside", Raymond Burr, at Whakatane.

Below: World record! Eve throws the discus further than anyone else at the Commonwealth Paraplegic Games in Dunedin in 1974. Her personal tally for the games: four golds and two silvers.

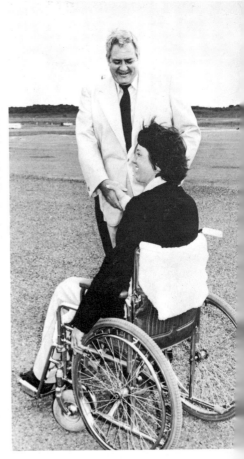

a kid I always resented the playthings I had; I always felt that I should have had a train set and that it wasn't fair that girls weren't supposed to enjoy such things. I guess there's something of me in Julie and Wendy, but I've always regarded it as a fallacy that boys and girls should enjoy different things. It totally depends on personality and it doesn't (or shouldn't) matter that some activities appear "sissy" or "tomboyish".

There's a great difference between the two girls, but they get along well considering these differences. They have their disputes, but that's typical of all kids.

When the house was fairly new, with the wallpapers (which I hate) still in new condition — that means bad news with little children — the walls in the hall were one day simply covered with scribbles. I've always been pretty liberal in what I've allowed the kids to play with, but I did exercise fairly tight control over where they used them — and this wasn't one of the places. Julie was old enough to know this but Wendy was still toddling, so it seemed that she was the culprit. However, Julie was at the stage where she could draw a full face, complete with eyes, nose, mouth and ears, more or less in the right places, and some of the scribbles included these faces, which meant Wendy couldn't very well have done them.

So I got them together and said, "Now, who did this?"
Julie promptly said, "Wendy did."

Wendy wasn't old enough to defend herself, so I asked her if she was the guilty party.

"No," she said.

I looked at Julie. "Are you sure you didn't do that?"
"Oh, no," she said. "Wendy did."

I said, "Julie, you've got to tell me the truth, otherwise I'll have to punish you in some way. There are a lot of things I'll put up with, but I won't put up with you telling me lies. And I won't punish you if you do tell the truth."

But Julie still insisted that it was Wendy and I knew jolly well that it wasn't. The biggest punishment I could think of was to forbid her watching *Lassie*, which had just begun on television and was the highlight of her week. I put her in the bath while the show was on and it nearly broke her heart. She cried and cried until I was feeling really sorry for her and ashamed of myself. But it worked. She finally admitted that

it had been her; or partly her because they had done it together.

"Well, I told her, "now you know. You're old enough to
know not to tell lies and now you've been punished for
lying."

Apart from the occasional incident like that, both of them
have been good as far as honesty goes. They're not afraid to
speak up openly with me, which means they are not sneaky
kids. They know my rules and they know they are not
difficult to abide by.

I've always encouraged them to have lots of other kids
around the house. When they were little there were times
when the whole neighbourhood seemed to be inside. The
floors would be literally covered with junk, and they'd all be
having a wonderful time. One of the favourites was mothers
and fathers — which at three and four I considered a pretty
harmless occupation — and I found one of the children from
down the road tucked up in a bed one day. I asked him what
he was doing there.

"I'm the baby," he said proudly. "Julie's my mother and
Wendy's my father."

I thought it was rather sweet. Julie and Wendy were both
snowy-haired little things. Their son was a Maori.

I guess other mothers thought I was out of my mind
allowing the kids to mess up the house the way they did, but
as far as I was concerned it was a clean mess and I didn't have
to worry about where my kids were and what they were doing.
Other kids still pour in and out of the house as if they live
here, and there's still a mess at times, but when you can't
chase around after your children yourself letting them make
a mess at home is the best possible alternative.

Here again, my childhood was much the same. Pop was always filling the house up with stray kids and feeding them,
and we always felt very free. We assumed that all houses were,
like ours, full of all kinds of people. We regarded it really as a
home, not a place where we lived under some kind of suffer-
ance, so we grew up without being made to feel a great debt
of gratitude to our parents for allowing us to live there. Maybe we took this a little far; whenever one of us decided it was
time to leave, we naturally wanted to take all our own stuff

with us, which included the bed, the chest of drawers and whatever furnishings we'd come to regard as our own. It didn't really occur to us, unless someone pointed it out, that these possessions were provided for us by our parents and therefore belonged to them. I went so far as to bring the piano with me when I moved into my own home because I considered it was mine. Mum had helped to pay for it, but I was the one who learnt to play it. She was rather upset when I removed it; she thought I might have asked, but it hadn't even crossed my mind that I should.

What I think about now, of course, is how I'm going to react when my children move out and decide to take their furniture with them. In a sense, it will be theirs because we bought it for them. Julie's bed is identified as Julie's bed and each has her own property in the sense that they are the users. This is important; a child must have things that are hers, but obviously there's going to come the time when we have to decide whether the attitude of possession that we developed can be applied as positively to our own children. Will I preach what I practised? Or maybe they won't ask.

People are constantly surprised by the level of independence of my daughters. This isn't entirely because I trained them that way but rather because, with that quick intuition that kids have, they soon became aware that they had to be. I could never carry them for instance, so therefore they never expected to be carried except when my sisters came visiting. If they wanted anything, they came to me because they knew I couldn't easily go to them. They didn't run away because they knew I couldn't chase them — and being chased is the whole purpose of running away.

Sometimes I would look out the window and see one of them bawling because she'd hurt herself or got into some conflict. I'd call out, "Come in to Mum" — and they were never so badly hurt that they couldn't. And they'd usually be so little hurt or upset that by the time they'd made their way inside they'd have forgotten what all the tears were about anyway. I used to see other kids let out a squawk of imagined hurt or a scream of anger and their mothers would be instantly leaping out the doors and picking them up. My kids soon learnt that where they were concerned this didn't happen.

But they were boisterous children. I sometimes feared to take them visiting anywhere where they would be let loose in someone's house and I wouldn't be able to control the situation. I didn't think it was fair to inflict them on others, so their visiting tended to be restricted to Mum's or Kel's mother's homes. Maybe they wouldn't have caused any problems, but I wasn't prepared to risk it. Maybe this was a throwback to my own habit of putting dampeners on my own visiting; but they had plenty of outings anyway. We were always going off to the beach, the lakes, the hot springs or other places. They learnt to swim as fast as they learnt to toddle — they were in the water at the hot springs when they were five months old, and loving it. They would jump fearlessly into the deep end before they could walk properly.

But they had to learn fast that when I'm in the water I can't stand up and my hands are fully occupied treading water. The worst thing they could do was cling round my neck. Wendy almost drowned me one day. She forgot and clung on to me and down I went. I thrashed around frantically trying to find something to hang onto and, unfortunately, clutched at a woman who was standing nearby and was quite unaware that my flounderings weren't just in fun. She was quite handsomely endowed above the waist, as everyone discovered when I grabbed the top of her swim suit and pulled it down. She was outraged, and I had to make hasty explanations to prevent her staging a major scene.

People found it difficult to understand that although I couldn't walk I could swim. We were at the springs one day after I'd spent many happy hours slapping red paint on my new canoe, a handsome plywood one which Kel and I built together when the original canvas one became so worn that only its paint was holding it together. Kel carried me to the edge of the pool and dumped me in and I had my swim. But as he was helping me back into the car afterwards, a man rushed over from a nearby group, anxiously asking, "Can I help? What's happened?"

We stared at him blankly for a moment. And then it dawned on us. He thought the red paint on me was blood and that Kel was helping me because I'd injured myself. We had a hell of a job convincing him that it was only because I was paralysed and couldn't walk and was spattered with paint; he'd seen me swimming in the pool and wouldn't believe it possible. When it did sink in, he was terribly embarrassed. I felt so sorry for him — he'd been so genuinely concerned — and it sounded ridiculous to explain that I'd been painting a canoe. I could see him thinking, "If she's paralysed, what the hell is she doing painting a canoe?"

These were the days before the abilities as well as the handicaps of paraplegics were widely publicised. Most people still thought we just sat around in wheelchairs or lay in beds. Like the time in 1972 when a man rang to organise me to go to the Bay of Plenty Sportsman of the Year dinner. When the phone went I was in the bathroom, sitting on the floor and painting happily with a roller. One of the kids answered and told the caller, "Mum'll be a few minutes. She's painting the bathroom." When I finally reached the phone, I could hear the puzzlement in the guy's voice. As I say, people do imagine you're lying around all the time or, at least, are startled when they discover you do the normal things, like painting bathrooms, that able-bodied people take as a matter of course. But if you think about it, sitting down and sloshing paint about is actually a damned sight easier than setting all the painting gear safely aside, dragging yourself on your backside out of the bathroom, across the hall, into the bedroom and up onto the bed to answer the telephone. Try it sometime and you'll see why I find painting — at least at the lower wall levels— quite simple. The fun bit in the exercise is levering yourself up on to the bed into a sitting position without any assistance from your legs at all.

I think my worst experience in coping with the kids was when Wendy was still a toddler. I was sewing in the sitting-room and Julie was at kindergarten. I knew Wendy was in the bedroom on my bed, and I knew that she loved to play with the taps over the basin alongside the bed; and I knew that I should get up and go to see what she was doing. But it is always such an effort to get up, so I just called out from time to time to ask what she was doing.

Each time she called back cheerfully, "Nothing."

After a while I came to the realisation that she must be doing something and that her innocent "nothings" were highly suspicious. But I wanted to finish that last little bit of sewing before tackling the next chore, so I stayed where I was a little longer. When I finally got up and went to the door, water met me coming down the hall over the brand-new carpet. The bedroom was completely awash. Wendy had put the plug in the basin, turned both taps on and then lost control of the situation.

Water had soaked through my bed and through all the clothing I kept on and in the window-seat and it was, really, flowing down the hall. Well, that much water had to go somewhere. And Wendy was standing in the middle of the chaos, saying rather unconvincingly, "I didn't do anything."

I managed to slosh through the flood in my callipers and turn the taps off but that was it. Anyone would have trouble cleaning that mess up; for me, it was hopeless. I had to admit defeat and put out a Mayday call to the family to come and help.

Another incident which wasn't quite so bad occurred earlier when I was still pregnant with Wendy and when Julie was at the toddling stage. Like my mother and her mother and probably her mother's mother, I had a great big bin in the kitchen for flour. Julie soon found that she could open this bin and play with the contents. I kept telling her not to; but this time I was in my bedroom having a rest and she was messing happily around the house. Everything was blissful peace, in fact, until I got up and went to the kitchen. Julie had baled virtually every ounce of flour from the bin onto the floor and was having a wonderful time in the middle of it.

My children's attitude to my disability was interesting. I am often asked what Julie and Wendy think about having a mother who can't walk. Well, the answer is simple: they don't think anything about it. Quite often they forget entirely that I am disabled and treat me exactly like any other person. I was always afraid they would be adversely affected, for instance through other kids teasing them. Kids can be cruel, and I believed they could be exposed to some unpleasant remarks about me. I imagined them going to school and being teased about a mother who couldn't walk, and developing the upsetting fixation that they had a mother who was "different" in a somewhat undesirable way.

No-one was more surprised than I was at the way it actually turned out. When I first took Julie to kindergarten, the other children rushed up and wanted to know why I couldn't walk properly and had these gadgets on my legs. Once I explained to them in simple terms, they just accepted it. I was Julie's mother and I had crutches and that was that. They were actually quite fascinated by the novelty, although perhaps if they hadn't met me at the outset their reactions might have been different. Kids can form strange opinions.

Julie had one bad patch when she moved from kindergarten to school. Here some other children must have said something to her because she came home in an upset state. She burst into tears when she saw me and clung to me.

"Oh, Mum," she said, "I wish you were like other mothers."

"Why?" I asked. I was alarmed because I had explained to her many times that it didn't make any difference and that, in fact, I had probably spent more time with my children than other mothers did with theirs. I used to sit and lie with them a lot, read to them and devote a great deal of time to sharing their interests and activities. And I'd always encourage the other neighbourhood children to come to our place to play. I'd thought they were pretty well adjusted to the situation, but now Julie was really upset.

She said, "I do wish you were like other mothers. I wish you could walk like other mothers. I wish you could run."

It dawned on me that she was upset for me, not for herself. I thought, "I'd better tread very carefully here because the way I react could be crucial in its effect on her." So I played it very cool.

"Julie, you know I've explained to you why I can't walk, what happened to me. But you know it doesn't really matter. I can drive a car. I can drive you to school and bring you home. I can take Wendy to kindergarten. I can cook your meals and sew dresses for you and keep the house clean. I can look after you and read to you and be a good mother to you. It doesn't really matter that I can't walk or run. I'd like to be able to, but it's not important. I can do just as much with you and for you as other mothers could, and probably I do a bit more as well."

She looked at me carefully and saw that it really wasn't

worrying me — I felt like crying with her in a sudden burst of pity for myself, but nothing would make me show it — and then she nodded suddenly and cheerfully, said, "OK," then ran away to play. She probably never thought about it again.

Because I was always conscious of the possibility of affecting them, I was always doubly careful about keeping them clean, looking after them and making sure they were well fed and so on. I didn't want to invite criticism. People would be very quick to say, "She shouldn't have had those children because she can't look after them," as soon as they saw the slightest evidence or even apparent evidence of neglect. I could be sure that anything and everything would be blamed on my disability — even a runny nose. Any of the other kids in the neighbourhood could have runny noses or be dirty, but it would never be blamed on the inability of their mothers to care for them. The fact that I had a physical disability would be the first thing to spring to mind to explain why my kids had grubby knees.

I had to always be a jump ahead because I could imagine remarks like that being dropped within hearing of the kids. I really took parenthood very seriously; I tried my best to bring them up in an intelligent manner. I don't know if I've succeeded, but they have developed a great attitude towards life and to my disability in particular. If I'm sitting with my feet up in a chair they want to sit in, they just pick my legs up and toss them somewhere else or slide underneath them. It's all very casual and matter-of-fact and this was the kind of understanding I'd always aimed for.

My sisters had always had great faith in my ability to cope, but when Liz came over for her visit from Canada and brought her two children with her, even she was apprehensive at first when I said I'd look after them while she went away for a few days on her own. She eventually learnt that in some respects I could handle her lively two-year-old son better than she could. He knew intuitively that I couldn't run around after him, so he didn't throw down the challenge as he would to his mother. Instead, he went along cheerfully with what I wanted.

Julie and Wendy were home on holiday when Liz decided to go away, and she assumed they'd be around to help me.

But when she heard them planning to take an early bus into Whakatane and spend the whole day there shopping, going to a movie and so on, she promptly cornered Wendy and suggested, "Don't you think you'd better postpone that trip until I come back? Wouldn't it be better if you stayed with your mother because she'll be here on her own with the kids?"

Wendy stared at her wide-eyed. "Whatever for? Mum's all right. She can manage. What's wrong with that?"

Liz told me about it and laughed. "I just didn't have an answer. Wendy was so flabbergasted, I didn't know what to say."

Needless to say I managed perfectly, and Liz's kids and I had great fun — and no problems. I think Liz had momentarily forgotten that I'd brought up two children of my own — on my own.

Julie and Wendy possibly take my degree of independence for granted because they are highly independent themselves for their ages. Their self-reliance and initiative developed fast once they began discovering the things I couldn't do for them or that they could do faster for themselves. It's shown up in their school work; their teachers have invariably remarked on their lack of a need for the guidance that other kids seem to require. I think they're normal, average, everyday kids, but I am pleased that for their ages they have this trait.

I think every mother should aim for this and encourage it. For instance from the age of three, kids are always wanting to help in the kitchen, whatever's doing. If you don't let them help at that stage, they're likely to lose interest and never learn; and when you do want them to help they're neither interested nor able to. I always regarded their keenness to assist as an eagerness to learn. When they were two and four, they would want to help me with the apple pie or whatever I was making at the kitchen bench. I'd be grinding my teeth at the thought of the mess they'd make, but I persevered with it — I never took the easier view that I couldn't be bothered — because I considered it was helping them to learn. I can understand mothers not being bothered because of the mess at the end, but I had more than normal problems cleaning up and I think it was worth it.

And there are harder tasks. For instance, cleaning floors and windows. Washing and ironing has never worried me — although it was a major physical effort until I was able to get an automatic washer-dryer when we sold our Edgecumbe home and moved to Whakatane in 1974. Vacuum-cleaning is a major problem. On callipers I either have to do it standing upright or sitting on the floor. There's no inbetween. I can't bend over to do things because bending over means falling over. It was easier for me to sit down and slide around on my backside. At least I couldn't fall. In a chair, the wheels spend all their time getting in the way of the cord. However I do it — and even though it isn't a big house — vacuum-cleaning means a good hour at the least of hard sweat.

Spring-cleaning I just don't look at, however much I might want to. I can't clean ceilings and walls, and cleaning windows is an exercise in cliff-hanging. I cling on with one hand and clean with the other and I'm always gripping myself on a delicate point of balance, which would be a continual strain even if I wasn't trying to polish glass at the same time. I can do the lower windows from my chair, but the rest means getting into callipers and getting out the crutches and putting on a real performance. It's simpler to let them get dirty.

While the kids grew up, I maintained my emphatic standpoint that wheelchairs were repositories for the old and useless. In fifteen years after my accident, no-one and no persuasion would get me to even contemplate having one. I didn't know then, of course, that a wheelchair could propel me into a whole wonderful new world of activity and participation in life — that, sitting down, I could become almost like anyone else.

Chapter Eleven

Whee . . . 1 chair

FUNNILY enough, I've never really regretted that I lived those fifteen years without a wheelchair. I know now how much easier it would have been, particularly during the years when I was either having or raising two children, but there isn't much point in being wise after the event. Perhaps I might not have been so determinedly independent if I had accepted a wheelchair earlier. I'll never know and I'm not going to worry about it.

My resistance to the chair lasted strongly right up until my introduction to the possibilities of sporting activities. It wasn't until then that I realised it was a way of opening another door, and that it wasn't just the useless and the old who used them.

Now, of course, being reasonably accomplished on crutches and callipers and also having a light chair to whizz around in, I have reached a happy medium, perhaps the perfect one. I still use the callipers, but there are certain chores — going shopping is one of them — which are so much easier in a chair. The callipers are now getting less and less wear, especially now we've moved to an older house which hasn't been designed with my problems in mind as the Edgecumbe house was. Even after fifteen years I still totter on callipers and I can't stand for any length of time. I fall over or begin shaking. It's far too great a physical effort to walk far.

Socially, a wheelchair is marvellous because I'm so relaxed, so mobile. On callipers and crutches, I always had to be careful where I sat because I had to look ahead to getting up again, and I couldn't do that unless the chair was stable and had arms. Even the act of sitting was difficult: the best way was to fall forward and then turn over. I literally fell into chairs. But that's hard on the furniture — particularly other people's.

My sister's visit with her two children — a girl of eight months and a boy of two years — showed me how much easier it would have been to raise my own two from a wheelchair. It was a piece of cake to handle those two. I have a safety harness which attaches to the chair, and I put this around the baby. She could stay happily in my lap for hours. I often moved around the house with her on my lap and the little boy standing on the footrests, which he thought was marvellous fun.

But while I was trying to live as normally as possible and refusing to accept that there were things I couldn't do until I'd tried for myself and learnt the hard way, I'd never given a thought to the possibility that there was any way I could get back into sporting activities. Since the accident I'd assumed that this part of my life, except for swimming or canoeing for pleasure and fitness — they gave me strength in my arms and shoulders which was invaluable to me in my everyday life — was over and done with.

But one day in 1967 I read a short article in the Rotorua *Post* about Jim Savage. I'd known the Savage family through friends of Ailsa's for some years, and I knew that Jim had had poliomyelitis, but I never connected his and my disability in any way. I didn't realise that we were, in fact, both paraplegics. Like me, Jim had carried on an active life. Disability hadn't been allowed to make much difference to him. He'd go out with other members of the Savage family and keep up with them, crawling along the beach or in the hills, whatever they were doing. Later on, when the paraplegic movement really got moving, he even took other paras on hunting trips with him.

Once he and I went off to Waihi for a Lions meeting. Jim drove to Edgecumbe and we put our chairs in my car and away we went. Near Matata, the bonnet came loose and Jim told me to stop in the middle of the road.

"The middle of the road?" I asked.

"Yes, it's too rough for me on the edges," he said. He rolled up the legs of his trousers and revealed several thicknesses of long johns. For convenience he crawls about a lot on hands and knees, and the long johns are for protection because, as a polio para, he still has feeling in his legs and knees. Anyway, he heaved himself out of the car, crawled to the front and heaved himself up on the bumper. He was hanging there when two cars came towards us. I'll never forget the looks on the faces of the occupants when they saw Jim. Obviously, they put us down as a couple of drunks.

A little later we noticed the temperature light was on and the car was losing power. We crawled on, but eventually hit an incline and were forced to stop. Jim did his hands and knees act again, this time to unfasten the bonnet and see what was wrong. And this time an ambulance arrived and stopped, and the driver came over to offer help.

"She's right," said Jim cheerfully. "Mind you, we might need your help later."

However the ambulance driver used his radio-telephone to call the Automobile Association, who came out, found we had a burst heater hose, made temporary repairs, gave us some water and enabled us to reach a garage.

I mentioned this episode in my talk to the Waihi meeting to explain why we were late arriving, and I'm sure they all thought I was exaggerating when I pointed out that these incidents were nothing to Jim because he often went into the bush deerstalking and had once shot three deer in a day.

Anyway, the Rotorua *Post* article quoted Jim as saying that anyone paralysed through an accident or polio was classified as a paraplegic and that there was a growing popularity in paraplegic sport. A small team had gone to a Commonwealth Paraplegic Games meeting in Perth in 1962 and another team travelled to Jamaica in 1966. Jim said he'd missed out on that one because our area had no association for paraplegics. The team had been confined to paras from Auckland and Dunedin, because, through Jean Curry of the Rehabilitation Centre in Otara (Auckland) and Father Leo Close, a paraplegic priest in Dunedin, these two areas had got themselves organised.

So Jim was appealing for local paras to join him in forming a club. It was all news — and interesting news — to me, so I rang him and asked him what it was all about. Jim was surprised to hear from me; he said he'd forgotten all about me because he hadn't associated me with being a para either. It seems incredible how little we knew about the condition only a handful of years ago. Remember this was as recently as 1967. We chatted about the situation and I asked him what I could do. He explained that paras were graded according to their degrees of disability, so that they could compete equally against each other. He said that he intended going to Auckland to attend practice sessions. He then offered to bring some equipment down to Edgecumbe for me to have a crack at. I jumped at the chance.

Jim arrived one day with a shot, a discus and a javelin, and we tried them out on the lawn. Jim felt immediately that I had a lot of potential. I had the basic strength, thanks to those years of struggling with callipers and crutches, and I was vitally interested because sport suddenly loomed as another exciting form of activity. All I needed was the basic skills to add to the strength. I was hooked. I had to get some equipment of my own and find someone locally who would be willing to coach me. I knew I'd need help there because I had no appreciation of the techniques involved in throwing the discus or the javelin or putting the shot properly. Just getting them a reasonable distance away from me wasn't good enough. If I was going to do it at all, I was going to do it properly.

I accompanied Jim up to Otara, near Auckland, and there for the first time I saw paraplegics en masse. I was amazed that there were so many of them and that they could be so vigorous. It was actually the first time I'd seen people being so active in wheelchairs, and it really opened my eyes. Were these people who had given up on life? I suddenly realised that submitting to a wheelchair wouldn't be a gesture of defeat. If I could be active from it, it was for me.

Various activities had been organised at the centre by Jean Curry, and I went round picking the brains of everyone I met. I wanted to find out everything I could about how they managed their lives. I found it intensely interesting.

Then we took part in sports practice, organised by Max Steward, who had been to Jamaica as team manager and coach. He gave us the fundamentals, but it was obvious that Jim and I couldn't travel to Auckland every month just to train. I had my two little kids and Jim was a family man with a fulltime job. We couldn't afford the time or the money to give up an entire weekend every so often. The weekends would be a lot of fun, but they'd be tiring.

I was like a wide-eyed kid that weekend, astonished at the range of activities paraplegics could become involved in. There's very little, as I discovered then, that we can't do apart from playing Rugby and other sports like that. Some able-bodied people, an Air New Zealand crew from Mangere, got into wheelchairs and played us at basketball, which can be one of the most exciting games you can watch between good players.

During the weekend Jim Savage told me a lot about hunting pig and deer with other paras in the hills around Kawerau. Four of them drove deep into a valley once and got themselves stuck. They didn't have any able-bodied people with them, and they'd left their chairs back in Kawerau, so Jim got out, crawled round the back and began digging the car out. He had to do it alone because the others were big men who couldn't have got back into the car without assistance. But he managed somehow. He always did.

I remember the excitement later when he got three deer in one day — crawling on hands and knees through a paddock of ferns with some friends. His dogs must have been well-trained.

Back in Edgecumbe, I asked around about anyone who might be able to coach me in field events. Ray Gurren's name came up. He was a teacher at Edgecumbe College — yes, we had one now — and a local Rugby representative, so I rang him. He said he'd willingly give any help he could, but added: "You realise, of course, that I know nothing about wheelchair sports?"

"That's all right," I said, "neither do I, so we're off to a good start."

By this time, I'd buried my inhibitions and borrowed a wheelchair from Whakatane Hospital. I was beginning to get used to handling it. And I'd already set my sights — the first national paraplegic games which were to be held in Auckland in 1968. They were being run at Otahuhu College. Many prominent sporting people like Murray Halberg and Les Mills were helping, and the games were to be opened by the Governor General, so it all gave everyone terrific incentive and a feeling of belonging to something of value.

Ray could afford time to take me out training only once or twice a week, but I had the basics in hand by the time the games were held. The worst of the terrible frustrations were behind me. The discus was the worst. Getting the right angle and the right flight was a monumental challenge. If I just sat there and used brute strength, I could get it just far enough to know I could not get it far enough to win anything. The discus is aerodynamic and needs relaxation combined with the correct shoulder and arm movements to achieve the correct flight.

Anchoring my chair was a major problem, because it would move as soon as I put any effort into my swing. We usually used someone as an anchor; he would have to fold himself down behind the chair out of the way of my arms and hold on hard. They use special chair holders in competitions.

The techniques of throwing the put were much the same as those used by able-bodied people — except, of course, that all the power has to be developed without the leverage of leg action.

Another problem was simply how to keep warm while sitting in one position for long periods. I used special exercises to keep my body temperature up while my coach studied my actions, someone acted as my anchor, someone marked my throws and others retrieved the shot or discus or javelin. As a teacher, Ray was able to get volunteers from the college to help, otherwise I don't think I would ever have got there.

Keeping my feet on the footrests was another problem we had to tackle from scratch. We're not allowed to put our feet on the ground. We also found it was necessary to strip as much of the wheelchair off as we could to give me maximum freedom of movement. The arms and backrest of my chair now detach, but initially I had a lot of skinned knuckles from hitting metal fixtures.

Ray knew all the theory of the various throws, and he patiently spent hour after hour, week after week, month after month trying to adapt his knowledge to give me a wheelchair technique that would work. At times I felt like chucking the whole thing in. I'd be almost crying with the frustration of not getting any better, of being stuck for weeks at the same distance. Then, suddenly, I'd pop one out a little farther, and we'd be encouraged to keep on trying. More

Eve and Jim Savage pioneered the setting up of clubs and social activities for paras. On this page: table tennis at Kawerau, and a wheelchair basketball match in Turangi between paras and able-bodied people. Ron Reid and coach Ian Brown in line.

"Youngsters today are bett[er] educated to the difficulti[es] and needs of the disabled.["]

Left: The loneliness of [the] long distance speaker. [At] another public speaking [en]gagement, this one at Wait[...]

Below: Eve with parap[legic] Nelson journalist S[...] Horrocks.

weeks, even three months, would go by before I'd suddenly gain and retain another metre or so.

Being me, thinking big, I knew I'd have to throw the discus at least 14.6 m to get anywhere internationally. And even at this early stage, although I still hadn't competed anywhere, that was where I wanted to get because there were paraplegic Olympic Games scheduled for 1968 and I had the bug to qualify. The games were to have been held in Mexico in conjunction with the able-bodied Olympics, but they decided they couldn't cope with the paras — I understand they could hardly cope with the other games — so Israel had offered to stage them.

The team was to be announced right after the nationals at Easter that year, so I didn't really have much time to get myself ready. My training hadn't begun properly until the previous June. I had the results from the games in Jamaica to give me an idea of what distances I'd have to achieve, but I had to work from rock bottom to get there.

At this time, there was no-one else in New Zealand to provide me with competition in my own particular disability class. Only two other girls — Gaylene Harris from Auckland and Louise Pentecost from Hamilton — competed in the 1968 nationals, and they weren't in the field events. And, in any case, they had different levels of disability. I was in class three, as I am now. The levels range from one, which is broken necks, through to six, which they're eliminating because it's for people who are only paralysed in the foot or something — really not much more of a disability than Murray Halberg suffered when he broke his shoulder and wound up with a withered arm, before he became an Olympic champion and world record-holder.

I remember the shock we got later when we reached Israel and the American team came bowling in, 100 strong. We were waiting for a lift at the time, but a whole bunch of them couldn't be bothered waiting — they suddenly jumped out of their chairs, folded them up and carried them off up the stairs. We sat there with our mouths hanging open — we'd had no idea there were paras who could walk around carrying their own chairs.

Anyway, those first nationals in Auckland were tough on

sole competitors like me. No allowances were made for us, so we couldn't gain a medal or any other recognition for what we achieved. This has since been remedied, but at that time we were penalised for circumstances which were not our fault. They held the preliminary qualifying throws on the first day and that night posted a list of those who had qualified for the finals on the second day. I'd had only three of the six attempts I was entitled to, but I wasn't listed. They'd just taken the top qualifiers from each grade except those in which there was only one competitor.

I pointed out the unfairness of this to Murray Halberg, who agreed and talked to someone about it, and I was finally allowed my other three attempts. I suppose this was just part of the teething troubles of getting the sport established in New Zealand, but I always felt that I, particularly, had to battle because I was the only woman and logically I would always win. However, to me, the winning was not as important as gaining every opportunity I was entitled to to qualify for overseas.

Anyway, I achieved my best throws at those nationals; my precision javelin was actually better than any other competitor's. So, obviously, Ray and I were working on the right lines, although I learnt a lot from watching the techniques of more experienced athletes and got wonderful help from Jean Curry. She was totally involved in the rehabilitation of paraplegics, had taken the first small team to Perth in 1962, was team physiotherapist with the Jamaica team and did everything she could to help everyone she could.

I went back to Edgecumbe and trained on madly to achieve the best performances I could before the team for the Israel Olympics was selected. And, finally, we sat and listened to the announcement of the team over the radio. Fourteen men were chosen – and one woman. Me. I'd made it.

I was spurred to even harder training schedules. Ray and I still had no guidelines to correct wheelchair technique other than those we worked out for ourselves by sheer trial and error. We'd test certain angles of arm, wrist and hand movement and all the possible variations of sitting and holding and throwing. If one didn't work out, we'd change to another. If that didn't produce the results we thought we wanted, we figured out yet another variation.

Paraplegics have a full training manual now as well as constant reference to the techniques that others have used successfully. There are so many competing now and we meet so often competitively that it seems hard to believe that only a few years ago there was nothing to help us except our own determination. Certainly there was nothing in Edgecumbe.

The shot, I found, was not too difficult because I had the basic strength to build on. The javelin was all right, too, because I had a strong throwing arm and I had always been a good ball thrower. Most women don't achieve very good javelin distances because they don't seem able to master the technique, which really whips it out. They don't throw with the wrist, but mine had become stronger and stronger over the years, mainly through canoeing and supporting myself on crutches. In that sense, I had a head start on the others. I felt strongly that all being well I must win the javelin in Israel — thanks to Jean Curry's information service, I knew approximately what the rest of the world was capable of.

And by this time Ray knew my capabilities pretty well too, and he prepared me efficiently for what lay ahead. Following his schedule and guidelines, I was in a fine state of fitness by the time we were to leave, although being a wife and mother didn't make it exactly easy to stick to the schedule. Kel and the girls were all most helpful and as keen as I was, but schedule training is a lot tougher on a woman than a man. I still had to plan and prepare meals and keep the house and the kids running smoothly — they were eight and six then and still in need of a fair amount of supervision, even though Mum and Pop were just around the corner to keep an eye on them from time to time.

Pop, of course, was busting out of his skin with pride. He'd always been sports-mad, and to have a daughter selected to represent New Zealand at an Olympic Games filled his cup to overflowing. Mum told me he scanned the newspapers every day, and if there was no mention of the paraplegic games or, specifically, me, he'd throw the paper down in disgust and say there was no news in it.

The day I left he was up at 5am, kicking everybody else

awake to make sure we were all at the airport in time. He was 86 then, and the last I saw of him as we took off were his bright pink cheeks and his walking stick waving a frantic goodbye. It was a great event for him and I knew he'd be boring everyone to tears about it. I don't believe in great emotional farewells, but this was quite a send-off. There were family, friends, relations and well-wishers. The Rautahi Maori cultural group had already given Jim and me a huge send-off in Kawerau during the week, and presented each of us with a Maori cloak and head-band. In deference to them, I chose these as part of my going-away outfit.

It was an excited, happy, hectic departure — and a relief to settle back for the flight to Auckland to join the rest of the team. I didn't think for a moment that I'd left disaster behind me when I flew away from Whakatane.

Chapter Twelve

Liquidity problems

IT was a small disaster to begin with . . . the housekeeper we'd arranged to come in to look after Kel and the girls didn't turn up for a week. Then Julie fell ill. Kel and the children coped all right, but if I'd known what was going on I'd have worried myself sick.

There was much worse, but I didn't find that out until much later.

The trip, of course, was my first away with a team. It was, very exciting, but it was educational as well for me because for the first time I learnt a great deal about paraplegics from many countries of the world. I love meeting people and observing their reactions and attitudes, but it was doubly interesting to get alongside so many other paras.

I can't speak highly enough of the coaches, trainers, handlers and others who travel with us on these trips. It's always a real performance to move us around en masse — getting us into an aircraft, for instance, is a major operation — yet everything is done so efficiently.

We were loaded at Auckland by a forklift that took two chairs at a time, then lifted by our escorts into our seats. This can be quite a task in a confined area like an aircraft cabin when you've got big fellows like Leo Close, the Catholic priest from Dunedin, who is virtually paralysed from the armpits down. They're very heavy and awkward to lift. I walked up the steps in my callipers because I thought I'd be able to move a lot more easily in the plane if I wore them. The theory worked out quite well, but I didn't take into account the swelling that would take place. We flew via Sydney to Singapore, where we were to stay for three days, and when I took my shoes and callipers off there I discovered my feet had swollen like balloons. I couldn't wear the shoes or callipers again that trip. Everyone had swollen feet, and this

proved a particular trial for us in the hot, humid Singapore
climate.

The flight wasn't without event either. I had a window seat
and, because I had my incontinence problem riding right
along with me, I was constantly up and down, which meant
that every time this happened the two men alongside me had
to get out of the way. They hauled themselves out, muttering
about "these bloody women", and I would then stagger off
along the aisle, hanging on to the seats to face the major problem of getting into the toilet. Even on big aircraft like the
DC8, you need a tin-opener. Imagine me, stiff-legged on
callipers, trying to sit down and get comfortable. The whole
thing was hopeless.

Once I tried sliding down the aisle on my behind, but I
gave that up when I left a wet trail behind me and the boys
all started throwing off about it. Really, it's impossible to
describe, except as a joke, what a bloody nightmare the problem was in situations like that. I didn't mind the remarks
— "That Eve, there she goes again" — "Gee, she's absolutely
hopeless" — "No control at all" — but when I finally put it to
them, "Well, look, you guys, you must be in the same fix", I
didn't get any satisfactory answers.

I hadn't had any real contact with other paras, apart from
Jim Savage — and he's a polio case. Polio cases don't generally
lose bladder control, can still have sexual relations quite normally and generally have none of the particular problems that
traumatic paras do. So, apart from my own specific experience,
I was totally ignorant about the whole question. I was still
the only paraplegic I knew really well.

The others on this trip weren't about to enlighten me,
either. I think New Zealand men are notoriously close-
mouthed about these things. They don't talk very easily about
personal matters, least of all to a woman. But when I realised
that I was the only one making all these trips and that the
men were enjoying themselves at my expense, I kept trying.
I asked a couple of them, "You fellows must surely have
the same problem. How the hell are you coping?" The answer
was completely evasive: "Well, of course, we're men and men
cope much better. You're weak, anyway."

The doctor had given us lots of notes about what to take

and what not to take and what to eat and drink during the trip; and he'd advised us to drink plenty of beer particularly when we got to humid countries because beer is good for the kidneys and, as a rule, water in eastern countries isn't good for anything. So when the drinks trolley came round, the boys piled obediently into the beer. I'd always been terrified to drink it because it went straight through; I stuck to what I found to be the most comfortable drink, like sherry, which would absorb into the blood stream and not add to my incontinence problem. But, obviously, beer would flood straight through the systems of these men, too, yet here they were downing great quantities.

I remained in darkness on the point until the middle of the night. Then our escorts went running up and down with little blue plastic bags, asking, "Have you got one? Have you got one? What about you?"

"Hey," I called — I wasn't missing out on anything — "Aren't you going to offer me one?"

Back came a laugh and the answer, "Oh, they're no use to you, Eve."

And the boys beside me finally enlightened me. They turned up the cuff of one trouser leg and there was a little valve on the end of a tube. The tube connects to a bag which straps round the inside of the thigh and the bag is connected to a sheath which fits over the penis. So all they had to do was open the valve, empty the thigh bag into the blue plastic bag, tie it at the top and leave it under the seat for collection.

"My God," I said when I discovered the little secret. "It's not fair. Why can't I have one of them?"

As soon as I could, I got hold of the doctor, Bill Liddell, of Christchurch. "Hey, Bill, couldn't you . . . ah . . . jack something like this up for me?"

Bill dashed my hopes pretty quickly. He explained that the only known female urinals were so hopelessly inadequate that they didn't work. This was because when you sat down, you sat on the outlet. I later found one and tried it. Bill was right; it was fine while I stood up but when I sat I blocked it off completely.

"Well," I asked, "what's the alternative? There has to be one. I mean, transplants are all the rage now, what with Dr

Barnard doing his thing in South Africa. How about one of those?"

Bill grinned, "Well, it's a pretty good idea. Eve, but you'd find it very hard to get a donor."

"Yes," I had to agree, "I probably would."

So we left it at that, although later Bill told me something about the system I now have. He was explaining how they train paras in the spinal unit at Christchurch Hospital to employ tapping procedures and external pressures to condition the bladder to empty at certain hours. He went on to describe a system involving a major operation which was still only partially accepted in paraplegic circles. The unit was performing the operation only when it was pressured into it, he said, although it was automatic for spina bifida children because they had to have it to survive. As far as performing the operation merely for the convenience of the para concerned, this depended on the particular doctor and the hospital, he said.

Anyway, when I finally arrived in Israel and found myself among hundreds of women paras, I was full of questions. I'd spent some time during the trip toying with the thought of the operation, but I rejected it as a last-ditch effort. I had never had a major operation my life, I was perfectly healthy, and I wasn't prepared to submit to surgery unless I absolutely had to.

But I had no solution and swollen feet when we landed in Singapore — and I'd lost my voice, too. One of the Air New Zealand stewards on the flight was a professional entertainer and he'd produced his guitar and helped us sing ourselves out of voice and sleep all the way. And I was carrying a tape recorder with the idea of recording my impressions of the whole trip.

The Singapore accommodation was excellent, and we had a comparatively good time, but we learnt an important lesson. Don't make a prolonged stop on the way to the games. Travel is tiring at the best of times, but three days in Singapore compounded the problem because of all the arrangements and functions in which we were forced to become involved. None of us could maintain the level of fitness we had when we left New Zealand.

One incident from Singapore sticks in my mind. We were at dinner in the hospital one night when an Indian doctor who, apparently, was a well-known alcoholic, swayed in, surveyed us all for a while and then suddenly waved his arms and cried, "You people can walk! There is nothing wrong with you!"

There was an embarrassed silence as everyone tried to ignore him, but he wasn't going to be ignored. He rambled on loudly that we were all victims of delusion, that our condition was only in our minds, and we had only to make the effort and we could all get up and walk like anyone else. Then he called for a volunteer from among us to prove his point.

We all looked pointedly at Rex Fattorini, who was sitting against the wall on the far side of the table from the doctor. "OK Rex," someone said. "You're it." Rex is a double amputee paraplegic. Both his legs had been removed because of spasm trouble which affected him after he became a para.

He got the message immediately, being the bright boy he is, and became the focus of all attention as he made a great show of wheeling down to the far end of the table and round the end, while the doctor eagerly waited for him. But as he rounded the table, it became quite obvious that he had no legs.

The doctor went berserk. "That's not fair!" he shouted. "How can a man walk when he has no legs?"

Someone among us quietly asked: "How can we walk when we're paralysed?"

Fortunately, red-faced hospital staff moved in then and led the poor chap away.

We joined a planeload of Australian paras for the Singapore-Israel leg. They'd claimed all the rear seats, which made it doubly difficult for our escorts to get us all settled, and meant my trips to the loo had to be made through their definitely cheeky ranks. By the time we hit Tel Aviv, the Aussies and Kiwis couldn't be called the best of friends. Matters weren't helped when a mix-up over our chairs ended with me sitting in one belonging to an Australian girl, who wasn't at all pleased about it.

By now, on top of the exhaustion, several members of the team were suffering from dysentery and associated complaints

like stomach cramp. I'd developed a bladder infection, something which hits me far harder than it would a normal person.
It was further proof — as if we needed it — that we should
never have stopped over in a place like Singapore. It was a
shame, because most of the team suffered the whole time we
were in Israel and were weakened considerably.

Bill Liddell had plenty of potions to cope with most of the
troubles, but I went a step further by immediately adding
skinned heels to my swollen feet. I was billeted in a youth
hostel in a small room with three double bunks — dreadful
accommodation compared with the facilities for the men. It
was on the second floor, the lift wasn't operating properly
and seventy-two of us, Japanese, Rhodesians and various other
nationalities, had to share three toilets and three handbasins.
You either got up at 4am to be first or waited until about
9.30am to be last. Oh, yes, and there was a bar directly
beneath us which stayed open all night and every night, and
was frequented by Argentinians and other enthusisastic
guitarists and singers and accordionists who liked to sing
and play until dawn. We slept all right until we got over our
exhaustion, but then we had no option but to get down and
join them — even if it meant tackling the exhaustion stakes
again. If you can't beat 'em, join 'em was the only alternative
to tossing and turning all night.

The floor of the ablution block was concrete, and the door
into it was so narrow it wouldn't accept a wheelchair. So I
had to hoist myself several metres from my chair through the
door onto the toilet seat. It was too wide a gap to jump
across, so I somehow lifted and swivelled myself over, a
contortion which meant my heels dragged across the coarse
concrete each time. They rapidly developed blisters, which
promptly burst and became raw sores.

So there I was, comfortably settled into Tel Aviv — with
my uncomfortable sleeping quarters, rotten ablution facilities,
lack of sleep, bladder infection, skinned heels, swollen feet —
but, somehow, I didn't miss a training session. Looking back,
it was a wonder I managed to compete at all.

I tried telling the men of the difficulties, but they weren't
particularly interested. I think they just thought it was Eve
moaning again and acting like a typical woman. I found it

better to shut my mouth and say nothing. I was already experiencing some rather bad emotional bouts — thinking about the kids and what a dreadful mother I was for leaving them on the other side of the world. And, of course, I was also prone at the time to menstrual problems, and that was something I couldn't possibly discuss with the men.

I was in fine shape to put up a creditable performance for my country!

The Israelis had converted buses to get us from the village to the stadiums at which we were competing. They were fitted with ramps so we could be wheeled inside and ride there without leaving our chairs. Trouble was, many of the chairs, including the Israelis', didn't have brakes. So as we bounced along the roads and swung round the corners we shunted up and down like railway wagons in a goods yard. If the truck stopped, we all hurtled forward and piled up in the front; when it moved again, we all shot to the back. I had to hold my bandaged, skinned and swollen feet up in the air to avoid further damage from all these stampeding chairs.

There was one good thing. The meals in Tel Aviv — lots of orange juice, cold chicken cooked in oils, tomatoes, bananas, beautiful fruit — caused us all to lose weight rapidly, but I have never had such a beautiful complexion before or since. I usually have a bad skin because of all the butter and stuff I eat in New Zealand. The Israelis, I might add, have lovely skins all the time.

I had five days training before beginning my competition in the swimming. I entered this only because we were all allowed six events but I hadn't trained for it at all, so I was flabbergasted when I took the silver medal. It took all my effort to cover the 50 m and I hadn't expected to come anywhere but last. Second was incredible. I was helped because the gradings and classifications used in Israel were the only ones I've experienced internationally that were completely fair as far as the swimming was concerned. They'd graded complete and incomplete lesions in separate events so that I swam only against other complete lesions in grade four, in which I was classified at the Games. As you can imagine, incomplete lesions have more movement and mobility which, particularly in water, gives them an advantage. Most polios were classified incomplete and I didn't have to go into the water against them, as I have had to do ever since.

My silver was the first medal for New Zealand and since it was so unexpected it was a great booster to a team rather down with its illnesses.

I had the preliminaries for the field events on the Friday and then the games closed down for two and a half days. Everything stopped at 3pm on Friday because Saturday was the Israel Sabbath and Sunday belonged to the Christians. Tours were organised, but because we knew how exhausting these could be those of us who'd made the finals stayed in the village and trained quietly and slept. You have to conserve energy if you want to compete seriously and, for me, tours and trips are out.

The nights eventually became a lot of fun. We had music and singing out under the trees and I made a lot of friends. The nationalities were well mixed up and got on well together in spite of the language problems. This intermingling was possibly the most wonderful part of the games for me.

Don't get me wrong. I like competing, and I like winning. I want to win. I always aim to equal or exceed my best performances. Then, even if I don't win, I get real satisfaction. But getting to know people, making friends, is a lasting pleasure.

We got on well with the Israelis. I took tobacco from New Zealand with me, and I used to roll my own cigarettes in the evenings. They were fascinated. Many of the older people who visited the camp had not seen anyone rolling his own since the New Zealanders and Australians fought there in the Second World War. I ended up rolling cigarettes on demand. Even the staff began coming along and indicating by gestures they'd like cigarettes the way I made them.

The language problem was fun. I tried to learn something of everything and found Spanish particularly intriguing as a language. A Spanish para named (naturally) Juan joined me at meal-times and we discussed our respective activities of the day. It took us about half an hour to blunder through this ritual and understand each other, but I was speaking the language quite well by the time the games ended. I used to think, Gee, that was a great conversation, even though neither of us got much out of the other. The fun was in trying. A lot of the paras, including some of our own, preferred to stick to themselves and not make any effort at communication, either because they couldn't get through immediately or they felt embarrassed. I think they missed out on a lot.

The Japanese girls were next to my room, and they were cute. They were so tiny and neat and rode around in little wee chairs. They became most interested in me when they found out through their interpreter that I was married and had had two babies since becoming a para. I was asked one night to join them and be interviewed by them.

"What for?" I asked. "What's so unusual about me?"

"Oh," said their interpreter, "we want to know about your marriage and your babies."

They did, too. They asked everything. They all sat there and shot questions at me through the interpreter and they didn't leave a thing out. I was handling questions on married life, children, sex. The big questions were: is it possible and, if it is, how? One girl had been married with a child of seven when she was paralysed in an accident. Her husband had instantly divorced her and taken the child away. She lived and worked in a rehabilitation centre where she'd become keen on another para, who wanted to marry her as much as she wanted to marry him. But she was desperate to know if it was going to work and if she could have children and so on. I assured her that she could have children and, if she could have children, she could certainly have and enjoy sex also.

Jim Savage told me later the same thing happened to him. He was cornered by the Japanese men and put through the same mill. They were great ones for learning and copying — every time we went training, they'd be there taking photographs and making drawings.

We had great arguments and discussions with the South Africans and Rhodesians. The general attitude was that we all had the right to compete against each other if we wanted to and no right at all to interfere with other countries' policies just because we didn't happen to agree with them. The way they run their countries has nothing to do with sport at all. In fact, sport helps to foster understanding.

Dragging politics into sport only reinforces the political barriers and makes the chance of understanding more remote.

Certainly, there was no detrimental effect from the mixing of nations in Tel Aviv. We had South Africans and Rhodesians at Heidelberg four years later — and again no problems, no intrigues. The problems that crop up in racial sport are created by people who aren't sportsmen. Since then a multi-racial South African team has competed at the international para games in England, so the problem that seems to dog the Olympics has been conquered by the wheelchair fraternity.

The only slight hitch, both in Tel Aviv and Heidelberg, was that when the Rhodesians arrived, the British, who of course instigated the games, insisted they should march under the British flag. The Rhodesians flatly refused and marched, with only a banner, behind the South Africans. They hadn't brought a flag with them in fact, and they told me it was because they didn't want to cause embarrassment. I commented that other people didn't seem to mind causing them embarrassment, and they replied mildly that they just didn't want to be instigators of problems. I think the British were a bit narrow-minded — the Rhodesians considered the games so important for the rehabilitation of their people they were prepared to forgo the right to carry their own flag — but it was really the only disagreement we experienced.

We learnt a lot from both Rhodesians and South Africans, particularly on sporting techniques and training. It was because they could contribute so much that they refused to let political and racial differences matter. There were only whites in the South African team, to be sure, but they seemed to get along fine with all the coloured people.

The preliminaries told me I was capable of winning medals in the field despite the setbacks I'd experienced. I knew exactly what I was capable of. But my shot put was disappointing because of the delay between the warm-up and the actual competition. I don't know why, but for some reason the officials walked away and left me after they had fastened me into the holding device. It was not only a nerve-wracking situation, it was also late, about five o'clock, and when the sun goes down in Israel the cold rushes in. So I had cooled off long before they returned and my best put was nowhere near my best. In fact my best distance at home would have won easily.

Another shot put incident was typical of the crazy goings on. One girl was in the circle and had marks out where she had put the shot. Before the officials measured her throws, they took the markers out. Her coach immediately came up shouting and carrying on, so the field judge put the marks back, where he thought they ought to go. This didn't satisfy the coach. He pulled the markers up and planted them where he thought they ought to go. A hell of an argument followed, but instead of making her compete again — which is what should have happened — they counted the marks where they had been finally put.

This was ridiculous. The ground was so hard the shots didn't leave a mark; and even if they had I would defy any-one to say correctly which marks belonged to whom after a whole bunch of competitors had been through the circle. We watched this performance in horror. The English judge was wandering about during the wrangle, but although he was sent for urgently he didn't arrive in time. Incidentally, the girl in-volved was the winner of the event.

I won the javelin, but it was with another fairly poor throw, again because of confusion about when we were to compete and when we should begin to warm up adequately.

But in the discus I achieved one of my best distances yet — mainly through rage. By the time I got to the event, I was so upset by the delays and the tactics of the opposition, which I felt were quite deliberate, that I was fuming with anger. Obviously the Israelis had by this time figured out who was the toughest opposition and their calculations included me.

When the Israeli girl went into the circle, her coach deliber-ately placed a mark for her to aim at. This was quite illegal, but we were helpless to do anything about it because the officials running the event couldn't speak English — or they pretended not to — and we couldn't get any protest through to them. With other competitors, too, they used delaying tactics. They would get them in the circle and walk off, leaving them to cool down while they drank coffee or some-thing. It was all quite ridiculous — and quite pointed. There was nothing our coach could do about it.

I knew that when I put maximum effort into my throw, I needed toe straps on my chair to hold my feet on the footrests. It was classed as an illegal throw if a foot slipped off. This was ridiculous, too. Feet have nothing to do with it. You'd be cheating if you could throw your feet off to help body movement; but it's a different matter if you are incapable of leg movement and your feet slip involuntarily. But to qualify for straps we had to produce a doctor's certificate saying we suffered from extreme spasm. Yet spasm wasn't my problem — it was purely the length of my legs. The movement of my upper body when I exerted maximum effort just naturally threw my feet off — after the throw was completed. It was particularly bad in the javelin because of the particular follow-through I had developed.

Anyway, I went out with toe straps on and the judge insisted that I take them off. A great argument in the circle followed between the judge, the doctor, our coach and various other officials while I sat there becoming gradually more and more unnerved. But instead of cooling off, I built up such a state of rage that I put out my best efforts yet, which took me from sixth place to third. I was delighted — I hadn't expected to win but I had been hoping for a place. The discus had been the hardest event for me to learn, and I hadn't really mastered it by the time I got to Israel.

Incidentally, they still applied the same toe strap rule in Heidelberg four years later — and I still think it's unfair. I discussed it with the Australian doctor, Dr Bedbrook, and he agreed it was a specific physical problem for me because of the length of my thigh and the flexibility I'd developed through walking on callipers. Logically enough, the bottom half of my body reacts when I throw the top half around.

The Australian team had strap trouble at the Commonwealth Games in Edinburgh. Some of them strapped the whole of their upper bodies to make themselves rigid so that they could use maximum effort without throwing themselves about. This caused a big argument. They insisted it was quite legal, but it had been decided in Stoke Mandeville that it wasn't. They competed with the straps on, and protests were put in by other teams, particularly the New Zealanders, and they had to compete again without the straps. Oddly enough, it didn't make a scrap of difference to their performances — which proved something to both sides — to the Aussies that

Help! What happens next? Eve Rimmer the disc jockey on a Radio Whakatane breakfast session.

The great Edgecumbe flood of 1970. Neighbours in the garden, with Eve's daughter Julie in the canoe. Eve and Kel were inside by the radio transmitter.

Two golds and a bronze at the home of para sport. The medal presentation at the Stoke Mandeville international para games in 1972.

Sir Ludwig "Poppa" Guttman, the founder of the world para movement, receiving a donation from New Zealand team captain Jim Savage at Stoke Mandeville. Eve describes him as "a wonderful inspiration".

they didn't need them, and to the rest that it didn't matter if they were used anyway. I used the same argument about toe straps — but so, still, does the opposition.

One of the South African coaches in Tel Aviv told us a great deal about their training methods. He'd devised a stand for propping paras up on their callipers so he could put them through all the normal throwing motions until they got the feel of what it was like. Then when he was satisfied with their movements, he put them into their chairs. As a result, he had very fine performers with beautiful throwing actions. He also had quite a number of them throwing out of the backs of their chairs, which were cut right down so they could turn completely and get a full range of movement. This was particularly useful for the shot, which they could bring right across their bodies, throwing out the back with a full follow-through. I now have a chair with detachable arms and back which gives me greater freedom of action.

One of the worst features of the Tel Aviv Games was that no medal presentations were held during them. Everything was kept until after the last event. Results were impossible to get hold of and, right up to the last, none of us was really sure who had got what or where. It killed the sense of achievement. Our coach Max Steward ran about trying to find out, but nobody seemed to know anything officially. It wasn't until the morning after the last event that he rushed in and said, "You've got a first, a second and a third." It was the first official result confirmation since the swimming — first in the javelin, second in the shot and third in the discus. I felt a tinge of disappointment because I had produced better marks in all events in New Zealand.

I still had a sense of let-down when I was presented with my medals. I suppose I shouldn't have been so upset about my distances; my coach had impressed on me the need to aim for consistency rather than for a best-ever throw. He'd told me that if I was regularly throwing 1.46 m I shouldn't expect to go overseas and get 1.52 or 1.58 m, which was my best, because of the travel, the exhaustion, the conditions, the tension and all the other factors. So when I went up to get my medals the main thought, in my mind was how pleased Pop would be. Gee, I thought, he'll be thrilled. I was visual-

ising his hearing or reading about it and I thought: this will
really make his whole year. He'll talk about nothing else and
bore everyone to tears.

I had no idea that he had been dead since before I began
competing.

Chapter Thirteen

Sad road home

THE day before we left Tel Aviv to head home, Norrie Jefferson moved me into the men's quarters, because some of the teams had already left, so I could spend the day in relative comfort. And that's when he came in and said he had a letter for me. He was sorry, he said, but it was bad news.

I thought, good God, what's Kel writing to Norrie for? I thought of several things in a flash of panic. My mother — I saw her falling down the steps; my children — they'd been run over or fallen from their bikes. The last person I thought of was Pop.

Norrie said: "I'm sorry, it's your Dad."

"It can't be," I said numbly. "It can't be Pop. Not him."

"Yes, he died a week after we left New Zealand."

Then he gave me Kel's letter and left me to it.

Wendy had replaced Julie as the sick one in the house, so Kel took her round to Mum's for the day and Mum greeted him at the door: "I think you'd better come in and look at Pop. I think he's gone."

Pop was lying in bed, holding a cowboy book open. The light was still burning and his glasses were perched on the end of his nose. He went to sleep like this every night, but this time he would never wake up.

It was so unexpected. The day before, he'd cooked a tremendous chicken dinner and had people in to share it. He'd gone to bed at his usual time and done all the usual things, putting his glasses on and settling down to read until he fell asleep. Mum had slept in another room for years because she couldn't sleep with the light on all night like he could. That morning she became worried when the lifetime habits were suddenly broken. Pop didn't get up at 5 a.m. as he always did. So she got up, and that's how she found him. He must have died almost as soon as he got into bed, because he hadn't got past the first page of the book.

It was fortunate that Kel turned up when he did. Mum was

distraught and he was able to take charge; but he was in a quandary about me. I was by then in Israel and beginning my competitions. Kel couldn't decide whether I should be told. Finally he did one of the wisest things he's ever done by deciding not to cable me. What would have been the point? I couldn't have done anything except get upset. If I caught the next plane home, I wouldn't get home until after the funeral; if I stayed on, knowing Pop was gone, I'd perform badly.

Instead Kel wrote to Norrie Jefferson, explaining what had happened and enclosing a letter for me as well, asking Norrie to break the news to me when he felt it was the right time.

Of course it never was the right time until the last day, when my part in the competitions was over.

Kel had written the best letter he's ever written. He doesn't write a lot, and this was only one page — just the facts beautifully said. But I still couldn't take it in. It took a long time to realise that he'd died not knowing I had won any medals. This was even more shattering, because I had pictured him as being proudest of all.

Everyone was very kind, but I cried, I think, all the way from Tel Aviv to Hong Kong. I sat next to Rex Fattorini, which was a good arrangement because my long legs need a lot of room and Rex, having none at all, gave me extra space. He was a great comfort; he let me curl up on him and, when I wasn't crying my eyes out, get some sleep. The doctor gave me some knockout drops, too, and these actually worked. I'm not a crying person normally, but when I do cry I think about all the bad things that have happened to people and I really let go.

The Heep Hong Club, an organisation for disabled children, met us in Hong Kong with special transport with a ramp which folded up to close in the back of a van in which we sat in our chairs. Unfortunately, as we climbed the steep incline to our hotel, one of the boys leaned against the ramp and it flew open and crashed onto the road. We were lucky all the wheelchairs didn't shoot out the back to provide a really spectacular arrival. But we had to pay for the damage.

The hotel was our moment of luxury on the way home. I shared a room with the physio Jean Curry and we dined in the Mandarin Room, a fantastic Chinese restaurant. We were told we could have anything we wanted, but the menu was entirely of Chinese dishes. I pointed out a few things and hoped for the best, but the boys clamoured for good old Kiwi tucker — we hadn't seen steak and eggs for three weeks — and got mad because they *couldn't* have what they wanted. Quite a few refused to eat anything. Consequently, they drank rather too much on empty stomachs and caused a bit of a scene.

I eventually had to make a hurried exit from this raucous stir. Someone passed a remark about me which incensed someone else, who insisted I should be treated like a lady, which triggered off a general argument about how I should really be treated. I can take just so much embarrassment, so I got out. Some of the boys went out later looking for their own kind of food and had all sorts of adventures tearing round the Hong Kong streets in their chairs. By that time, I was in bed.

We took part in paraplegic games organised at an air force base at Kowloon. They were well run, but their main problem was that the walking paras were doing everything from a standing position. We explained they'd have to sit in chairs if they wanted to compete internationally. But apparently this message didn't get through because the next time we saw them, at the Stoke Mandeville Games in 1970, they were still a team of athletes who performed best standing up. When they were forced to sit down in chairs they were hopeless. But once they did get the idea, they were fast learners. Ten of them were at Heidelburg in 1972 and they did extremely well.

As in Singapore, there was rather a don't-care attitude towards the Hong Kong paras. We were asked to go back if we ever could to help them, but we've had to be content to do what we can from New Zealand. I'd like to go over there and work. I feel I could make quite a contribution. There's a large number of paras there — as in New Zealand they're not sure how many altogether, but they're getting more and more of them out of their corners and involved in useful activities.

I knew that when I got home there was going to be a lot of publicity about my success. Norrie forewarned me to pull myself together and I knew it was going to be an ordeal. But it was still a great relief to get back on to Air New Zealand. I could have kissed those stewards — they were really marvellous. They insisted that I eat — I wasn't hungry, but they kidded me into it. Because we were now catching up on time again, they were serving meals every two hours or so. Still, it was a distraction and helped me to push thoughts of my father into the background.

Because I was the team's only medal winner as well as its only woman competitor, I was at the airport for five hours before I could get away. All the media, including the television news and "On Camera", wanted interviews.

Kel and my sister Ailsa came through the barrier to join me. I told them I'd get through the session if they didn't mention Pop. I felt sorry for Jean Curry, too, because she'd had a cable telling her that her mother was ill and she learned at the airport that she was dying. She went all to pieces. I felt like doing the same. But I survived and I drove home next day, picking up the pieces of all the disasters as I went.

Looking back, I know it would have been foolish for them to have told me all these things while I was away. There would have been nothing I could have done. It would have been a terrible waste of all the money and effort that had gone into getting me over there. It's one of those difficult situations where you know that whatever you do is going to be criticised, but I'm convinced in my own mind that the team management did the right thing. Nothing I could have done earlier would have made any difference to Pop. It couldn't have helped the family much, but it could have prevented a lot being done in the way of publicity and understanding for the paraplegic movement — which was, after all, the greater good.

Chapter Fourteen

All gold and go

I WAS in a zombie-like state when I got home, and there wasn't much immediate relief. First we had to attend a terrific civic reception in Kawerau, with bands and marching girls and a Maori welcome — the whole New Zealand-style bit — followed by a community welcome in Edgecumbe. I didn't expect that at all, but Edgecumbe had cause to celebrate. Warren Cole, who then lived in the same street as I did, had just won a gold medal with the Olympic rowing four in Mexico and the dairy factory had won a gold medal for butter production. So thanks to the three of us, Edgecumbe was on top of the world. Someone even composed a song for the occasion.

I had quite an adjustment to make because I still couldn't accept that Pop was no longer there. Mum was now on her own, and I was glad we were living close to her because she was badly afflicted with rheumatoid arthritis. I found it difficult to settle down to life in a small township after the travelling and excitement of the trip. This has been one of the most trying aspects of my life ever since — gearing back down to what is virtually a village situation.

However by this time Jim Savage and I had formed a club for paras in Kawerau, and we set about expanding the movement. We wanted to get clubs going all through the central North Island. We'd heard about paras in Tauranga and I was phoned by one of them. She was Rae Gibbs, who'd just shifted up from Palmerston North and didn't know any other local paras but had heard of me. We got her started and she became one of the country's leading paraplegic archers, specialising in the sport and doing extremely well at it. Jim found a para in Mt Maunganui, near Tauranga, so we moved in on that area and encouraged a club into activity. We made the clubs open to all disabled people as a social outlet and ran socials every month, with bowls, table tennis and so on. Tauranga has since gone from strength to strength with quite a large membership and a lot of helpers.

Hamilton already had an association representing Waikato, but we established a club in Rotorua and began rounding up support in Gisborne. Then I was asked to speak to several Napier service clubs interested in sponsoring a paraplegic association. The Junior Chamber of Commerce eventually took it on as a project and did a marvellous job. It now has a membership of sixty, including the people from the home for the disabled at Pukeora, near Waipukurau.

I'd already had some connection with Pukeora through ham radio. I used to talk on air to a Peter Garvey, who suffered from a rare wasting disease which had affected several male members of his family. He was a very bright lad until he was about sixteen, but he was about my age when I got to know him and he was slowly but surely dying. He fought on a lot longer than he was expected to, but finally succumbed about three years ago. I formed a great affinity with him. His speech was badly affected — he sounded as though he was drunk and was difficult to understand, which must have been terribly frustrating for a man so intelligent and alert. This damned disease was progressively wearing him down, and it was almost as painful for me to experience as it must have been for him.

He used to write the most beautiful letters, using an electric typewriter, but his movements became more and more limited. But they set him up at Pukeora with a radio room, and several others got interested and also got tickets to go on air. This was marvellous for them, because it was a contact with the rest of a world that had almost ceased to exist for them.

I used to talk every day with Peter and another Pukeora contact, Bubby Pomana, who remembered me from Cook Hospital in 1952. He was there because he'd dived off the Wairoa River bridge when he was fourteen and broken his neck. We saw each other only once at Cook, which was silly, because we should have been together, and we spent a whole year there at the same time. We could have helped each other a lot.

It was about the time I linked with Pukeora that we had a ham net that came on air every morning called the SIR group — the Sick, Idle or Rich. It was difficult for me at the time because I had the kids to look after, but every time

If I did send out a CQ I'd have umpteen dozen coming in on my frequency — either keen hams trying to be first to get a QSL card from me for their collection or young fellows wanting to talk to a girl.

My sisters often joined me in the radio shack — that room under the tank stand at my parents' home — and we picked up some real characters. I know this is deviating but I must put this guy in.

He called himself Romeo and he had a beautiful voice — charming and very debonair. He was a real lady's man. He talked to us a lot and told us one day he'd be coming up our way and would like to call and see us. We were agog about this. Ailsa was a very attractive girl, and she flipped when he told her to be ready for him when he called. We had a mental picture of him already. We knew he was a bachelor, and although we'd no idea of his age we saw him as a really gay young character (I'm using "gay" in the original sense) just right for our late teens. I was then twenty-one, Ailsa was sixteen and Elizabeth thirteen.

Anyway, one day this balding, aging gentleman knocked on the door and announced very quietly that he was Romeo. "You're what?" we chorused. All we could recognise was his voice. It was shattering — but it also turned out to be very nice. He was terribly shy, not at all like he was on the air. This is why ham radio is so wonderful for people who are lonely or inclined to be withdrawn. When they can talk without having to face the people they're talking to, their personalities change completely and they can really get something out of life that wouldn't otherwise be there. Anyway, Romeo remained charming.

But — back to Pukeora. I didn't get down there until after I was married and had a family. We were visiting the area, and I decided to call on Peter and the other hams. It was a minor nightmare because the kids were still little and Kel had to spend most of the visit chasing them round the home.

I was horrified to discover that a number of residents were actually much fitter than I was. I staggered in on callipers and crutches among many who had nowhere near my level of disablement. My first thought was: what the hell are they doing here?

I was, of course, very anti this type of home. I couldn't have stood the rules and regulations. They are run by hospital boards and I suppose the rules are necessary, but to me it was all too coldly institutional. Since then, I'm glad to say, they've changed a great deal for the better.

It was years later, after I'd become involved in para sport and been to Israel, before I went back to Pukeora. I was asked over by the auxiliary guild which looks after the needs of the people there to speak at their annual meeting. I took everything I had, including one or two films and my slides, talked to the meeting and then stayed overnight in the home and saw as many of the residents as I could. I felt as though I wanted to chop myself up into thirty pieces to talk to everyone, because they were all so interested in my activities. Yet to me they were living a life of isolation.

The home is in a very lonely place. It was originally a tuberculosis sanatorium and, obviously, when it was no longer needed for that, the Government decided something else had to be done with it. So they filled it with these disabled people to free some beds in general hospitals. I think it's extremely wrong to isolate disabled people in that environment. I was horrified there, and part of me wanted to get away quickly.

They asked me to stay an extra day or two because a bishop who was going to be a speaker at an Anglican women's function in Waipukurau the next night couldn't turn up and they thought I could take his place. I said I didn't know what the bishop would think about it, but that I would do my best.

Since I had the extra time, I showed all the Pukeora residents the films and slides, gave them an address that was at least three hours long and then was kept there talking with them for the rest of the day.

The greatest thing in favour of Pukeora was its most wonderful view. But I noticed they never looked at it. They all had their backs to it, physically and mentally; the interior of that house was their life. They looked in instead of out and they weren't rehabilitating themselves because there was no incentive. I'm not criticising the running of the home, either, because they had a school and workshops and everyone was suitably occupied. But the concept was wrong, the home was in the wrong place and the people in it belonged to no community but their own.

I feel very strongly that disabled people should be absorbed by the whole community. They should be able to wheel down to the shops, for instance — yet at Pukeora the nearest shops were at the bottom of a 5 km hill. So while I was there I got in touch with some of the local sporting bodies and asked if anyone would be interested in taking some equipment up to Pukeora and organising a sports day.

One of the women from a club, Shirley Verron, came up and we arranged as much as we could. Everybody had a go, although it took some of them up to ten minutes just to hold on to the shot or javelin or discus, let alone try to throw it. The incredible concentration and effort they put into it was an eye-opener for the staff. The physiotherapists were absolutely amazed by one person and said to me later, "Do you know, in all the years that fellow's been here, that's the first real effort we've seen him make." He was so keen and so thrilled by his own efforts that I said, "Well, he proves my point. If someone is given the incentive to want to do something, he'll make the effort and do it."

That was their introduction to active sport. Since then they've been absorbed into the Hawke's Bay Paraplegic Association and become very involved. What really pleases me is that now they get out of Pukeora a lot. They have special transport, and they travel out to challenge people in the local towns in bowls and other activities. They've sent teams to the national paraplegic games and to many of the local sports meetings. Once they had to get special leave, but now the administration has recognised the value of their participation and the residents are regarded by everyone as more or less normal human beings. Living in Pukeora is no longer like living in a jail without bars.

The nationals that year were in Christchurch, which was doubly interesting because Christchurch is the home of the paraplegic movement and the base from which a huge amount of unstinting work has come from national secretary Jim McKee and chairman Jim Milner. From them stemmed the organisation's many forms of help in sport and the general welfare of paraplegics and other disabled people. At this time I was serving on the national council as an area delegate, so I had the annual meeting to attend as well as the games. I was also able to get my first look at the work of the national spinal unit at Christchurch Hospital. I met many new paras just out from the unit and a lot who were still patients. They were able to come out to watch the games and get some real ideas on what they might be able to do as part of the rehabilitation.

Several Canterbury paras met the North Island contingent as we arrived at Christchurch airport; with them was a tall man who walked up to me, stuck his hand out and welcomed me on behalf of the city. This was my first meeting with Bill Uttley, specialist in spinal injuries in Christchurch. I was frankly amazed that a man of such importance with such a heavy workload could or should find the time to come along and act as a baggage boy. Later I found other people of equal importance at the boarding school where we stayed, making beds, preparing food and cheerfully doing even more mundane and less mentionable tasks. But this, I have learnt over my years in para sport, is just part of the wonderful comradeship that forms between paraplegics and the people dedicated to helping them back into the normal world.

I enjoyed my time as a national councillor. I never felt that any of the time spent on executive work was wasted by anyone. The rewards and satisfactions were many because we were able to help so many people up and down the country who otherwise would have had to battle on alone. And it strengthened my association with Father Leo Close, the paraplegic priest from Dunedin, who had always been one of our main spokesmen and was one of the most inspiring men I have known. It was a tragedy for the whole paraplegic movement when he died.

Involvement in para administration helps paras, too. It improved my understanding and appreciation of the problems of people other than myself — for so many years I'd been the only one who seemed to have my problems — and it widened the horizon of people like Peter Cooper, of Pukeora, one of my old ham friends, who became publicity officer for the association and did a great job. He also acted as delegate for the southern North Island centre.

The games in Christchurch were highly successful for me. I won the indoor bowls, the club throw, the javelin, the freestyle swimming and the breaststroke, and threw world records of 6.66 m and 12.62 m in winning the shot and discus. Considering my first competitive throws only a year earlier had been about 5.77 m and 12.09 m, I felt I'd come a long way in a short time.

We decided after these games to form a central North Island association linking clubs in Waikato, western Bay of Plenty, Kawerau and Rotorua to co-ordinate and strengthen our sporting, social and fund-raising activities. Here too we seemed to have come a long way in a short time — from being a few paras scattered about on our own to a respectably large unit with a voice in the national administration.

Chapter Fifteen

From Scots to Scotland

KEL and the kids were able to join us for the 1972 national game in Wellington, where we were billeted in Scots College dormitories — which was perhaps prophetic for those of us competing in the Edinburgh Commonwealth Games later that year. It was a significant meeting. Quite apart from the incentive of games selection, there were a lot of record performances which marked the fast improvement in the sport nationally, and we enjoyed a volume of television, press and radio coverage we'd not experienced before.

When the team was announced for the Commonwealth Games and the preceding Stoke Mandeville international games, I wasn't the only woman. In addition to ten men and me, they also selected Hamilton swimmer Louise Pentecost and Auckland archer Gaylene Harris. Not all the men were ex-Israel veterans, either, which again demonstrated how our sport was advancing and expanding. Actually the team could easily have been larger but we were strictly limited by finances.

It did promise to be highly successful. We'd learnt from our Israel mistakes, we were generally using better training techniques and we planned to reach Stoke Mandeville in good time to get over travel fatigue before we were flung into battle. And we weren't going to ruin things by resting along the way.

In fact we thirteen Kiwis, in battle against about 1,000 paras from all over the place, were to win, between Stoke Mandeville and Edinburgh, twenty-one gold medals, twenty-three silvers and twelve bronzes. And I was to be free of all the traumas that, retrospectively anyway, blighted my trip to Israel.

While I was away, my family was well-fed and well-cared for. When I'd made a speech at Wairoa before I went away, the people there offered to do something for me to help out, and as a result engaged the W.D.F.F. home-help service to look

116

after the family. So the home-bound Rimmers enjoyed the care and cooking of, first, Mrs Fairbrother, and then Mrs Hill, who reckoned it was the best home-help job she'd ever had because her charges were all so capable of looking after themselves.

We flew the Pacific to Los Angeles for a one-night stopover. The LA fog was appalling, and we slunk through it in an incredibly long six-door station wagon to our motel where our manager George Thorne, from Dunedin, discovered that our wheelchairs wouldn't fit through our room doorways. The management punched panic buttons all over the place in the hunt for rooms with wider doors, but the problem was eventually solved and I got on my bed immediately and stuck my feet up the wall. I may have looked odd, but I wasn't going to go through that dreadful swollen feet act again. The technique worked like a charm. We were all so tired we gave sightseeing a miss and early in the morning were off over the North Pole to London without seeing much more of Los Angeles than its endless overcast. The 747 that took us to London was a delight — a ramp for the chairs, a special chair inside that fitted the aisle so we could be wheeled to our seats instead of having to be untidily carried and — good news for incontinent paras — there were loos all over the place.

We all settled down happily to watch the in-flight movie, but when they sold us the earphones for the sound they omitted to tell us they were screening an old Charlie Chaplin silent. Even international air travel has its share of suckers.

The only real flaw for me was a screaming toothache which developed as soon as I left New Zealand and persisted all the way. I had all the other travel problems beaten, but I hadn't reckoned on that one.

But there was a bonus at the end of the flight. As we stacked up for the landing, I could see an Air Canada flight going in below us — with my sister Liz on board. She'd flown across to be with me in England and Scotland. It was a long time though before we got together. Paras in wheelchairs take a lot of sorting out, and then Rex Fattorini and I got stuck in an airport elevator. Liz just had to stand around and bite her thumbs for quite a time.

She followed the team to Stoke Mandeville and got lodgings in a lovely fifteenth century pub with fifteenth century plumbing and twentieth century tariffs. Quite apart from the fun it was for us to be together so much, Liz proved a wonderful extra helper for the team — and paras can always do with extra helpers.

My tooth was still giving me hell, and Sir Ludwig "Poppa" Guttman, the great founder of the para movement, gave it a personal once-over and diagnosed an abscess. The Stoke Mandeville dentist cheerfully and efficiently extracted it — the first and only tooth I have surrendered.

Poppa, incidentally, was a wonderful inspiration; his whole life has been given to the help and restoration of paraplegics, and he lived and slept by the principle of "do it yourself". Woe betide the para whom he spotted getting wheelchair assistance from anyone when it wasn't strictly necessary. You'd hear his bellow of censure right across the centre. At the same time he was the most understanding and gentle man, and he endeared himself to hundreds of Kiwis when he later visited New Zealand. I can't imagine any para under his care failing to respond to the challenges that life throws at people in our situation.

If Liz's fifteenth century accommodation had its oddities, ours wasn't much better. We were bedded down in enormous army huts, sixty to each, very cramped. Clothing was draped over the rafters, and there were some of the most ancient hospital beds I've seen. It was in such contrast to the fantastic Stoke Mandeville stadium. This had been opened only the year before and included an indoor pool, table tennis and basketball facilities and a seven-chair lift. It was flanked by a huge marquee for fencing and weightlifting, as well as large fields, a track, a slalom course and bowling greens for the strictly outdoor events. Everything had been designed for wheelchairs, so it was a bit like being in a paraplegics' heaven. Except that the beds weren't exactly cloud nine.

There were about 1,000 paras there from all over the world — there would have been more if there had been more accommodation — and against that lot our little squad did well — nine golds, eight silvers and eight bronzes. I got a gold and a record in the javelin, a gold in the shot and a bronze in

The world's leading paraplegic field events athlete in action at Stoke Mandeville—the shot, the javelin, the discus.

It was worse in the aircraft cabin. Special facilities for New Zealand para athletes and their wheelchairs overseas. *Above:* a special forklift device lifts Rex Fattorini aboard Air India transport in London. *Below:* The "Heep Hong" bus in Hong Kong. The ramp folded up at the back.

the discus. I finished feeling that I could hold this form for the Commonwealth Games to follow.

Altogether, Stoke Mandeville was an experience in paraplegia that I'd like to repeat, but finances have so far prevented us from going back there. It was a constant thrill to be in the birthplace of para sport and medical welfare and to meet all the wonderful people who staffed it and the volunteers who turned out in hundreds to help us — there were a lot of RAF personnel there and, I understand, many prisoners from a nearby jail. Many of these helpers — apart from the prisoners, of course — always timed their annual holidays to be available for the games.

And when the accommodation got too much, it was sheer joy to wheel off into the lovely Aylesbury countryside and spend time in one of the several charming pubs within wheeling distance of the centre. At first I couldn't figure out the vast difference between English and New Zealand countryside; then I realised it was the absence of roadside fences. Reserves open to the public seemed to stretch for miles.

Most of the games were well organised, although the field events, run by overseas visitors, were constantly interrupted by arguments and discussions about the rules and regulations. The medals presentation was an unfortunate anti-climax — an old table was dragged out into the grounds and the medals were dished out without ceremony or occasion.

We discovered there was no charge for our accommodation, so the New Zealand team had a whipround and gave Sir Ludwig a small cheque to help with running costs. We thought they needed all the help they could get as far as accommodation was concerned, and I understand vast improvements have been made since.

Leo Close had arranged with friends to be driven to Edinburgh, so when the rest of us crawled out early to catch our BEA flight, he snored on. This wasn't what some of the team considered a fair deal. So they dragged his bed, with him trapped in it, out into the early morning sunshine. They gave him hell while the bus was being loaded, but he wasn't at all upset and was still happily and comfortably lying there when we roared off.

Edinburgh, where the able-bodied games were just coming
to a close, really turned it on for us: a welcoming committee,
uniformed escorts and a fantastically well-organised bus
operation to get us all to Turnhouse RAF base where, after
the grim realities of the Stoke Mandeville barracks, the two-
man centrally-heated officers' quarters were luxury. But my
early impressions of Edinburgh — myriads of streets with
houses stacked together like Coronation Streets — made me
thankful for the New Zealand cult of the quarter-acre. We
viewed everything, of course, through the Scottish mist —
a thick drizzle falling endlessly from a heavy overcast —
which stayed with us just about all of the time.

We were in time to see the closing ceremony of the able-
bodied games at Meadowbank Stadium and discovered that
the Aussie para team had been there right through. They'd
bypassed the Stoke Mandeville games, a move on which
Poppa Guttman had expressed a dim view to us and on which
he later expressed the same dim view directly to the Aussies.

We got a special wave from Princess Anne when she passed,
inches away, with the rest of the Royal family, and then
outside we were treated to an even more interesting close-up
royal view as we watched members of a Highland regiment
boarding army trucks. Our raucous shouts warned them that
we had discovered, with the aid of the whipping wind and
the high truck tailboards, just what Scotties wear beneath
their kilts; the balance of the force climbed awkwardly abroad
with two men to hold their kilts down while a third gave
them a hand up. One thing about wheelchairs, you get an
interesting low-angle view of many aspects that able-bodied
people miss out on.

We were both amused and disappointed to observe that the
news teams covering the able-bodied games for New Zealand
took off in droves when the games closed down. As a result
we were given no special coverage at all — the news that
trickled back was once again so sketchy as to be almost non-
existent, despite the fine achievements of the team. We tended
to perform slightly below our Stoke Mandeville levels because
of the cold, the extra travel and the fact we were all probably
over our peaks, but we collected a little more than our share
of the goodies. I picked up two golds and a silver for my per-

sonal collection, but the drop in standard showed in my distances —6.11 m for the shot which I'd put 6.59 in Stoke Mandeville, 13.44 m for the javelin compared with 14.17 m and 13.52 m for the discus against 14.02 m.

The opening ceremony was unfortunately marred by rain and by a microphone which gave Prime Minister Heath trouble at first in declaring the games officially open. He was virtually speaking to himself and it was rather funny to watch his mouth opening and shutting without any sound coming forth — like telly with the volume off. We'd all paraded first along Princess Street past the towering castle in our special buses — converted Edinburgh double-deckers with the chairs downstairs and the escorts riding on top. This comfort and the wonderful warmth of the people helped a lot to make up for the lousy weather.

We behaved ourselves well in Edinburgh, although there was one night when things got a little out of hand. The Lord Mayor attended a reception at Turnhouse and, of course, there was no beer, only champers and other bubbly. The Aussies and Kiwis, being Aussies and Kiwis, drank it as if it was beer so the results were somewhat disastrous. I wound up on the mat. I had problems with a friend who was slightly under the weather — it's a problem getting someone out of a car, into a chair and then into his quarters when he insists on going to sleep. So I was rather late into my bed and, unfortunately, my little indiscretion was observed, reported and duly made the subject of a stern rap on the knuckles. However, when I explained my Good Samaritan performance, my sin was regarded with rather less severity than it might have been.

The games were followed by a mini-Highland Games, and some of the New Zealand athletes stayed on to take part. But following the able-bodied games and our own meeting, it was an anti-climax because there was so little spectator interest.

Our tears of sadness at having to leave Edinburgh and the many friends we had made rapidly turned to tears of frustration because we couldn't get out anyway. Fog forced us to wait many long, boring, empty hours at Edinburgh airport, and they were finally planning to shove us in buses and take us to Glasgow when a plane sneaked in and lifted us out and away to a comfortable London hotel and a magnificent reception thrown at New Zealand House by Sir Denis and Lady Blundell. Here we were all reduced to tears again when one of the staff joined our para Reuben Ngata in singing "Now Is The Hour" in Maori, a guaranteed way of bringing lumps to New Zealand throats when home is a long way off.

Because we'd had to send all our luggage, apart from a small case each, on via Rome to Hong Kong, some of us had embarrassing shortages of personal supplies for that old para problem. Lady Blundell was wonderful in this crisis: without fuss or bother, she sent out and had what we needed brought in.

On the way home we had great fun as tourists in such glamorous places as Rome and Hong Kong — where we played a team of paras at basketball and were soundly beaten.

At the end of a long, tiring flight to Brisbane, we had to sit it out in the plane while other passengers disembarked and all the regulations of various departments were carried out. Our escorts were glad to get out and stretch their legs, but our team coach Ross Macfarlane stayed behind with us. We were all hot, weary and pretty well-drained of our sense of humour as we waited it out as patiently as we could.

Suddenly a large uniformed official appeared and barked: "Right, you lot, everyone out!"

We looked at each other, then all eyes focussed on Ross as he slowly rose to his feet and asked quietly, "What's the trouble, mate?"

"Everyone leave the plane right now — this minute — and get a move on," replied the official in his best Australian twang. "I'm sick of people taking bloody advantage of me — the rule is everyone off!"

Ross now pulled himself to his full height, all of 1.83 m and very athletic: "These people can't walk. They're paralysed."

"Can't walk, be damned. That's what they all tell me. I'm sick of being made a fool of. Now, everybody *move*!"

Obviously we looked quite normal to him. We all had our limbs (most of us anyway) so maybe he honestly felt we were having him on. But our big weightlifter Bill Lean had an aisle seat near the official and I could see him flexing his muscles.

It's a great insult to any para to be told he can walk when he knows he can't, so most of us were holding our breaths in case Bill took counter-action.

Rex deflated the situation suddenly and dramatically. To get a better view, he decided to do his usual act by reaching up and hanging from the luggage rack. A legless man hanging like that is a startling sight, and when the official spotted him you could almost hear the penny drop. His face became an absolute picture in changing tones of dead-white and blood-red.

"Ah, um, gee, heck, I'm sorry," he stammered. "Of course, you must be the paraplegic team. Yeah . . . I've got lots of paraplegic friends . . . know them well, I do . . . great fellows — now then, you just stay right where you are . . . cheerio . . . see you . . ." and he was gone in a cloud of apologies, leaving us to laugh ourselves the rest of the way home to New Zealand.

And that was the end of a marvellous trip. I arrived back in Edgecumbe just in time for a major crisis on the home front.

Chapter Sixteen

The end of the floods

JUST three days after I got home from Edinburgh, Edge-cumbe had its great flood. The Rangataiki River broke its banks, and flood waters marooned the town. I was still trying to recover from jet lag and general travel weariness, but there was no time to relax. As the district vanished under water and then Edgecumbe itself began slowly submerging — at its height the flood lapped the top of the terrace outside our living room — the Civil Defence Organisation mobilised all ham radio operators to keep communications going, and since we were in the middle of the crisis the Rimmer house became the operational centre for the immediate area.

We maintained constant contact with headquarters in Whakatane and Auckland for three days and nights. This was an emergency we had trained for, and special equipment was brought in so we could work the emergency frequency and keep the rest of the world informed on what was happening in inundated Edgecumbe.

The real danger came when the Te Mahoe dam engineer had to let hundreds of thousands of cusecs of water go in the middle of the night because the lake build-up from the torrential rains in the hills which fed it was threatening to collapse the dam completely. So a virtual tidal wave burst down the river — big enough to have wiped Edgecumbe out altogether if the river hadn't broken its banks higher up and spread the water across the farm flats. We were lucky; instead of slamming solidly into the middle of the town, the flood sneaked all round us and came in by stealth.

All the phones were out, and we in the Rimmer house were about the only people who knew Civil Defence was planning a mass evacuation of Edgecumbe. To avoid a panic, we decided not to tell anyone unless it became absolutely necessary. Kel and the kids kept an eye on a fairly extensive area of the town by launching the canoe from the terrace and paddling across roads, gardens, and lawns that were feet below the surface.

I had the transmitter rigged up beside my bed during the emergency and on the night of the crisis, when we heard the dam had been let go, I was determined to stay awake right through, but at about 5 a.m. Kel let me drop off to sleep. I awoke in a panic demanding to know what I had missed.

Two radio operators sent out from Whakatane to give us some relief during the day nearly didn't make it. The roads had vanished so they tried a short cut across the park at the back of the house. They were nearly across when the woman next door spotted them and managed to attract their attention with frantic waving and shouting. She got them to go back just as they were about to step into a 2 m deep and fairly fast flowing drain.

Just as it had risen, the water receded again at an incredible rate as soon as the downpour that fed it stopped. But it left many Edgecumbe homes and businesses and much of the surrounding farmland badly damaged. It was the worst flood the district had known, and it led to a reshaping of the river and improved stopbank systems to prevent it ever happening again.

At the same time I began to do something positive about my own flooding problems. My return home with more medals caused an increasing demand on my time for speaking engagements, but late in 1970 I got myself down to Christchurch for a urological assessment which I'd discussed at Stoke Mandeville with Dr Bedbrook and Bill Liddell. I was intensely interested to see the operation of the spinal unit, headed by Bill Uttley, Bill Liddell and Jack Cunningham, the surgeon, with a trained physiotherapy and nursing staff for the complete treatment of paras.

A small urinary tract operation was performed on me, but this wasn't entirely successful, and I was given the option of submitting to a full ileal loop operation or staying pretty much as I incontinentally was. The ileal loop operation would eliminate the incontinence problem completely, simply by diverting everything past the bladder and connecting the ureter into a stoma through the stomach wall to which a fitting, complete with a cap and bag, could be attached. It was a major operation, which was why it was left to me to decide. Maybe I was a bit of a coward about it, but I didn't make up my mind to have it until after the 1971 nationals in Dunedin.

These nationals involved me in a bit of a contretemps. Because I was the only class four woman competing, it was ruled that I couldn't win a medal unless I broke a record. Since the records were already mine, they were fairly safe. The result was that I returned home with a single certificate and wasn't even listed in the official results, which showed only gold medallists. I was the only competitor to suffer from this remarkable ruling, but the other paras were just as furious as I was. According to the meeting records, I wasn't there. We held a meeting later and got it sorted out, successfully arguing the principle that a single competitor should not have to break a record to be noticed — it should be only a standard.

Apart from this, the weather was cold and miserable for the meeting and I suffered extreme discomfort. I was wet up to the armpits most of the time — and that decided me on the ileal loop. Anything, I thought, even a serious operation, would be better than that. It helped my decision that I was able to discuss the operation with girls who had had it successfully; as they explained it, it looked relatively simple.

So in May 1971, after visiting Wellington to deliver a paper on paraplegic sport to a sports medicine conference and to address the New Zealand health, physical education and recreation conference, I flew on to Christchurch and checked into the spinal unit. I chose this time because I calculated I should be fit enough to train fully later for the Heidelberg Olympics.

The operation was drastic all right, but I know now that it was worth it. Once I got used to handling the actual fittings and the problems of applying the cap and bag to the stoma, the difference in my life was just unbelievable. The stoma, incidentally, is rather like a small rudimentary penis on my stomach and, left to itself, just piddles away happily into a collecting bottle rather like a small hot water bottle with a valve at the other end for emptying purposes.

I was in Christchurch for three weeks. Quite early in my stay, the ham radio world found out, somehow, that I was there and a dear friend ZL3CP Charlie came in and looked after me faithfully every day, even installing a transceiver so I could talk to home at night. There was consternation in the hospital when Charlie began stringing aerial wires everywhere to get maximum reception. He was even told off by the fire service for draping wires across a fire exit, but Charlie didn't care too much. He's one of those dear souls, totally unselfish with his hobby, and he was a wonderful comfort. For the first time since my accident I was able to drink unlimited quantities of fluids without suffering dire after-effects. I could almost watch progress as it flowed in one end and out the other into the collecting bag.

I got back home still wearing my stitches and I was unable to do much in the way of housework or looking after myself or anyone else. Whakatane Hospital came to the rescue by providing a home help for some weeks and sending medical supplies. It was bliss to be able to relax on the terrace and soak up the sunshine without having to worry about keeping myself decently dry by dragging myself into the loo at regular intervals.

For the first time in nineteen years, I could wake up in the morning dry and not have to completely change my bed. My sheets actually got dirty for the first time. That made me the proudest person in town. And my sex life was greatly improved.

And then, to complete my independence, my escape from incontinence and all its unpleasantries, the era of the Janola bottle was born. It has been an inescapable item of my personal belongings ever since. Where I go, my Janola bottle goes also.

I'd better explain that. My little attached collecting bag isn't bottomless. Obviously if I'm out anywhere it's going to fill fairly smartly. I could go off to the loo to empty it out, but it's much easier to carry an overflow receptacle in my bag — and empty that less often and more conveniently. The plastic Janola bottle was the first choice — I can't recall why — and it's been a Janola bottle ever since.

I vividly recall watching from a distance at a Rugby function as the club president, walking past my bag where I'd parked it, noticed the Janola bottle. He stopped, stared at it, then bent down and picked it up. He shook it and sniffed it, most puzzled. I couldn't help thinking it would have served him right if it had not been empty at the time.

Anyway, armed with my friendly bottle and my ileal loop, I could drink anything, go anywhere, be comfortable all the time. Now I had to go to the toilet only every second day for other reasons. And Kel, with typical ingenuity, devised a workable drainage device that I could attach myself to at night. Apart from the occasional leaking flange or broken seal, I was suddenly blissfully leakproff. It was a drastic change for the better. But I don't madly recommend it to all paras. It depends entirely on problems encountered before and after the ileal loop is formed — there can be rejection problems — but for me it is the perfect solution. It was even better than discovering the advantages of a wheelchair. Learning those took time; this was instant.

It took about three months for everything to settle down and accept the changes made in my system, for the skin to accept the external fitting; and another three months for me to get back into full training for sport. This was plenty of time to get myself fully prepared for the 1972 nationals in Hamilton, even though I had now branched out into the pentathlon as well — the shot, javelin, archery, 60 m wheelchair dash and 50 m swim, all scored on a points basis the way the able-bodied pentathlon is — and therefore had to think about a lot more things and get a lot more done.

The Whakatane Archery Club co-operated in this expanded programme by inviting me to practise with them, and I got huge encouragement from a great archery enthusiast from Hawkes Bay, Bert Crispin, who also made me a bow.

I qualified for the pentathlon, so after the nationals I was selected to compete in that as well as my three field events in Heidelberg. Only ten were chosen, including two other women, Heneti Morgan, a charming Maori quadraplegic from Wellington, and Neroli Fairhall, from Canterbury, who competed in field events, slalom and dash.

After the experience of the anti-climax in Edinburgh, it had been decided not to follow the able-bodied Olympics at Munich, but to hold them before them and in another centre. They couldn't have made a better choice than Heidelberg. And the wisdom of the decision was underscored by the dreadful Munich debacle; our meeting could never have followed that horror. We enjoyed the most wonderful and inspiring games in Heidelberg, and it shattered me when I heard what happened in Munich.

Chapter Seventeen

Klaus, Henry and Albert

WHAT did I know about Germany before I went there? Not a great deal, I guess. My main impressions were what I'd got from Pop from the Second World War and from the general attitude in New Zealand. I discovered I had, as do most New Zealanders, certain basic misconceptions. Certainly, when we arrived at Frankfurt I found the first Germans we dealt with were full of precision, officiousness and even pettiness, but in Heidelberg, with more time to get to know ordinary people the friendships I formed with Klaus, Albert and Henry have become some of my treasured memories of a glorious city and a marvellous Olympiad.

We were the first team to arrive, and were welcomed in a magnificent rehabilitation centre called Beresfodesbundes-werk. I've never seen and undoubtedly never will again see a more superlative centre for the disabled. Not only were the buildings beautiful; their facilities were ultra-perfect. We all had single rooms with electronic doors and with every fitting designed for the disabilities of the people who used them. Pushbutton windows and blinds were operated from a bed-side control; there was FM radio, an intercommunications system, individual specially-designed baths and showers and loos. One escort, curious about the pull cords which hung about the place, pulled one and was instantly inundated with anxious Germans wondering what the emergency was.

The only flaw we Kiwis discovered was that there were no coffee or tea making facilities in the bedrooms. But I soon acquired what I wanted, which brought me into delightful contact with Henry. Henry was a speech therapist at the centre, a big, severe, unapproachable-looking man who never seemed to smile. He was in charge of the games' dining room arrangements and stood inside the dining room directing everyone with the solemnity of a traffic officer. He pretended to know no English, and when I told him about my need for a hot water jug, cups, tea, sugar and so on for my room, replied stolidly, "Of this, I know nothing."

130

But when I got back from training next morning, everything I wanted was there in my room. When I next pointed out to Henry that I would need milk, he looked at me and said, "So a jug is missing from the dining room. I know nothing of this. " And when I tried to thank him, he repeated, "I know nothing of this. Next thing we have the Chinese making noodles in their rooms and everyone cooking."

In this attitude, Henry was typical — the Germans generally were completely generous but they didn't seem to want anyone to know it.

Albert, who worked in reception, became a firm friend of the Kiwis because, being first in, we got to know him better than most others. He spoke little English and I know almost no German, but our friendship developed to the point where he kept me supplied with lovely ice-cold beer, with "danke schon" and "bitte schon" flying in all directions.

I had a hilarious conversation with him one day as I wheeled through the reception area.

"Eve," he called. "New Zealand Bier, wie ist das?"

Not quite understanding, I replied, "wie ist das?"

"Ja, wie ist das?"

"You mean, what's it like?"

"Ja, wie ist das?"

"Oh, well, it's fairly weak," I said. "Not like German beer — one bottle and you sleep all afternoon. New Zealand beer is . . . like Wasser."

"Like Wasser? Nein, nein, nein," responded Albert.

"What do you mean, nein, nein, nein? New Zealand beer is like Wasser."

'Nein, New Zealand Bier nicht Wasser," he insisted. "Ist like horsepiss."

He announced this with such loud authority that he stopped a foyer full of people dead in their tracks. And then he repeated triumphantly, "Ist like horsepiss."

Suspiciously, I asked, "Who told you that?"

"Oh," replied Albert happily, "New Zealand boy . . . he tell me your Bier ist like horsepiss."

At the next New Zealand team meeting, I asked who had given Albert this information. Everyone roared — I think I was the last in on the joke. I suggested however that someone had better correct him as he seemed to think it was a proper New Zealand word to use. And the management had a few cross words to say on the subject, too.

Klaus I got to know through my habit each morning of calling a good morning to the world over the intercom. He always answered and eventually, of course we met and became good friends. He was a lovely-looking man with a lovely wife, who he proudly introduced to me.

I met Albert's wife too and they were helpful in many ways. I had 100 marks to spend, but my one visit to the shops told me most things were expensive. Albert got me to explain about a dirndl (a skirt) I wanted to buy for Wendy, and his wife bought it for me. They took me once for a drive — in a VW of course — and at one stage Albert stopped the car and said he'd show me why the Germans didn't like the occupying American troops. There were a number of young American soldiers on a riverbank, drinking, throwing their beer cans in the river and generally appearing to behave in a totally disorderly way.

"They have been here too long," Albert said. He'd fought in the war, lost all his family and was now bitter about the continuing presence of the Americans because he felt they were doing no good for anyone. It was an interesting view of the other side of the coin.

When the time came for us to leave Germany, the hardest thing was to part from these so-called unapproachable, reserved people.

Highlights of the stay were evenings spent in a beautifully-preserved eleventh century castle, to which we bounced in our chairs over rough cobble-stones to listen to music and once to see a display of fireworks, which left the Orientals for dead. The fireworks were hidden all over the castle and the surrounding hill, and you couldn't imagine anything more startling. One night the Stuttgart Radio Symphony played Strauss waltzes for us, a thrilling performance in an exquisite setting.

On the other side, we experienced some thunderstorms which were the most violent I have encountered. But for the games the weather was hot and dry, and I was able to put in good performances, especially in the pentathlon, in which

I competed a week after we arrived. By this time we had all put jet lag and other travel hang-ups behind us and we produced our best efforts. We also made good use of excellent training facilities, for which all the equipment had been donated.

The games were held about 5 km from the centre at the University of Heidelberg. The fields, gymnasium, pool and other facilities were all together and the United States and German armies provided excellent transport for us. Our medal collection wasn't too bad — I won the pentathlon and shot and was second in the discus and javelin; Heneti was third in freestyle swimming, Graham Condon second in the discus, Jim Savage second in the shot and Graham Marriott third in the pentathlon and second in the discus.

A feature was the demonstration of a New Zealand-designed and made wheelchair holder for the field events, which we displayed with the idea that it could be adopted for all para games.

We couldn't stay on in Europe for sight-seeing after the games, although the New Zealand ambassador did take us for a trip down the Rhine before we shuttled on a long, jading flight to Hong Kong (where the local paras thumped us at basketball again). Still, we did learn to eat with chopsticks. We flew to Perth with Malaysian Airlines which, like most smaller airlines, gave fabulous service, and were delighted to find it was raining there. After the sticky heat of the East, it was fun to feel the rain in our faces. Our stopover included a visit to the Perth spinal injury unit, an up-to-the-minute and very complete rehabilitation centre 80 percent funded by the West Australian Government.

Coming back into New Zealand, I was astounded at the vigilance with which Agriculture Department officials checked our sports equipment. They inspected it and rubbed it item by item, but never once asked about our wheelchairs and where they had been. I just hope the holds of the aircraft where they were stored had been thoroughly sprayed. I may add in explanation that we always wore gloves when we went wheeling in Hong Kong.

It had been a wonderful trip — not least because my new irrigation system had worked beautifully, especially in flight.

Neroli Fairhall and I had shared a 2 litre plastic container between us, and for once I felt I had enjoyed mastery over mere males.

Eve Rimmer, B.E.M., with Ian Campbell at the investiture.

"The front castor rammed his foot deep into several inches of quality carpet." Eve, the Governor-General — and a wheelchair.

"Our medal collection wasn't too bad." Golds for Eve in the pentathlon and shot, and silvers in the discus and javelin at Heidelberg.

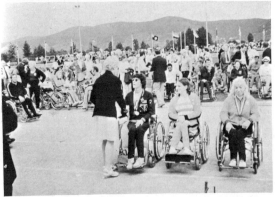

Eve receiving one of her gold medals in Heidelberg.

Below: Gold medal coming up. Eve competing in the shot final at the Heidelberg Olympics. The New Zealanders demonstrated a locally-designed wheelchair holder for the field events.

Chapter Eighteen

Another kind of gong

I WAS no sooner home from Heidelberg and awaking from a 17-hour sleep of sheer exhaustion, than I found Dairne Shanahan and TV's "Gallery" team on the doorstep, wanting to do a profile on me and my family. We spent that night talking about what we'd film and relating various crude jokes, while Dairne mapped out a shooting schedule. Next day, Kel took the day off work and we set to. It was fun all the way. We kept getting carried away with what we were talking about and the cameraman and sound technician kept getting involved too — because they weren't supposed to be seen or heard we many times had to cut and start all over again. They wanted shots of me hanging out washing, vacuum-cleaning, doing dishes and so on. Since I refused to sham anything, I got a lot of housework done that day.

Over the following days, Dairne reported several times from Wellington on her producer Des Monaghan's progress in editing all the footage. She told me that because I was to be on the same programme as Rob Muldoon, who was then Minister of Finance, they'd have to cut my time back, and they were finding it difficult to know what to throw away. This made me worry about what they might finish with. I find it embarrassing to watch or listen to myself, and can't be all that objective. But when they finally ran the programme, I was most impressed. And I was amazed to find they'd left in most of the bits I was sure they would have taken out — such as detailed discussions on incontinence and so on.

I learnt later that many paras who saw the programme were embarrassed by it. They lived with the incontinence problem but they didn't want people to know about it. And people apparently began making funny cracks about puddles under wheelchairs. I was blamed, although I had had no intention of embarrassing anyone — I was speaking solely for myself. It was a personal programme on me, but I heard later that it was widely taken as a programme on paras in general.

I was only facing the facts of life as I lived it. But at least it made a vast number of people aware of paras and of the benefits of sport and the ability of the paralysed to lead normal lives.

Soon after the programme was run, I went up to speak at the Ponsonby Rugby Club's Rugby Personality of the Year dinner in Auckland, at which Rob Muldoon was also a speaker. I was met at the airport and taken to the Monument Travel Lodge in Otahuhu, where I had 90 minutes to rest before being picked up to go to the dinner.

At 6.30pm, there was a tap at the door and there were not one but two uniformed chauffeurs.

"Madam," said one, poker-faced. "Your Rolls awaits."

"My what?"

"Your Rolls, Madam."

And it did. It came originally from the Queen and now belonged to Cliff Trillo, who owned the reception lounge which was hosting the dinner and who used it for special occasions and important guests. I felt most honoured.

Well, I've been in and out of hundreds of cars but this one nearly stumped me. It's a long climb up to the back seat.

"Look," I said to the chauffeurs, "this is going to look a bit undignified. I hope you don't mind."

I had to swing myself from my wheelchair into a sitting position on the floor of the Rolls and then hoist myself up into the seat. Getting out again was equally inelegant — I slid down onto the floor and then hurled myself down into the wheelchair waiting below me. Which rather took the gloss off the luxury feeling of sliding along the motorway like royalty.

I met Rob Muldoon for the first time over pre-dinner cocktails. Our introduction produced a remark from me which has been widely misinterpreted since. I happened to comment, "You're not such a bad-looking bloke, after all," which produced a roar of laughter from him but which has since been rendered as "You're not such an ugly bugger as I thought."

Rob took everything in great style. We had a great discussion on various political subjects and personalities, and discovered that we had at least two things in common — a sense of humour and a habit of outspokenness. We got on well together.

"But do you realise," I said, "my father would turn in his grave if he knew I was talking to you. He used to turn purple when he saw you on television."

During my talk I stressed that like all sports teams paras had trouble raising money. I made the suggestion that the Government might help by using its Hercules transport aircraft for ferrying sports teams, which would also be valuable training experience for the crews, and went on to talk about the difficulties and indignities we faced in trying to finance ourselves through raffles.

At this point someone, who was apparently rather inebriated, jumped up at the back of the hall and shouted, "OK, you've spoken long enough."

There was a shocked silence, into which I said, a little nervously, "Well, I'm sure Mr Muldoon won't mind, because he stole some of my time on television last week."

The man jumped up again, surprisingly announced that he'd like to start a travel fund for paraplegics, rushed to the front of the room, and plonked $10 in front of me. It began an amazingly spontaneous reaction. I hadn't asked for funds, but dozens rushed forward and began throwing $5, $10 and $20 notes in front of Mr Muldoon. I could see his eyes light up as the pile grew larger.

"I'll count," he said gleefully, "and you can take it with you. I'm good at this."

He was fending off lots of corny cracks about tax-collectors, but who cared? When we toted it up, we'd been given more than $600, which I sent off to the national association for the next para team tour overseas.

When my two-chauffeur Rolls Royce dropped me back at the motel, I was wondering if it had not all been a dream. What was I doing floating about in a Rolls Royce and coming home with $600 in unsolicited donations?

Another surprise followed — I was offered the award of the British Empire Medal in the 1973 New Year honours in recognition of the work I had done for the movement as a whole and for the promotion of rehabiliation through sport. I'd earlier been honoured by the local Old Boys football club

with the Bay of Plenty Sportsman of the Year trophy, which
was presented to me at a function in Tauranga by the previous
winner, Whakatane Olympic rower Wybro Veldman. It has
since been won by another para athlete, Ross Hynds of
Tauranga. It's wonderful to see para sport breaking through
with recognition alongside able-bodied sports.

Then the Olympic rowers won the New Zealand Sportsman
of the Year trophy for their gold medal in Munich and I was
placed second in the voting. Still, there weren't many individual performances of real merit that year.

So the honours were coming thick and fast. It made the
1973 nationals, held at Otaki at Easter in foul weather, something of an anti-climax. No one could perform well in those
conditions. However, it did attract many new competitors,
including some old friends from Pukeora, who were taking
part for the first time.

And then my daughter Julie, now at Edgecumbe College,
became junior athletic champion for the year. The following
year she was selected for the New Zealand secondary school
championships, held at Queen Elizabeth II Park in Christchurch, as a junior shot putter.

Word finally came setting the date for the investiture at
Government House in Wellington. It set me something of a
problem because each recipient is allowed to invite two
guests. The whole family wanted to be there, but we couldn't
afford either the time or the cost of all going to Wellington.
And my mother was then suffering in the advanced stages of
rheumatoid arthritis and couldn't possibly have made the
trip. It was finally decided I would go on my own and invite
two good friends of the para movement in Wellington, Ian
Campbell, now Wellington para chairman and a member of
the Accident Compensation Commission, and his wife to
accompany me.

About this time I got a phone call from Tauranga from an
Auckland journalist, Garth Gilmour, who'd been talking to
Norrie Jefferson about the possibility of a book and now
wanted to talk to me. He didn't even know where Edgecumbe
was, but he found it that night. We talked about the book
and, when the problems of the investiture came up, he offered
to take me through to Wellington and, on the way back, to

Turangi for a para field sports day and a talk to a local organisation that night.

So a few weeks later we launched the book away to a flying start by carrying a tape recorder in the car as we headed for Wellington so that I could talk as Garth drove. The tape recorder, of course, wouldn't work, so we just enjoyed ourselves by talking about what we could have talked about.

Wellington turned on one of its better days for the investiture — with a howling gale threatening to blow the impending rain right through us. Hats were blowing down the drive and expensive hairdos were being ruined as we arrived at Government House with Mr and Mrs Campbell. I was thankful for a short hairstyle and no hat — I had nothing that could be ruined. I was hauled up the front steps, and an aide took me into the ballroom ahead of the rest to check whether I was going to be able to negotiate the presentation obstacle course. This involved climbing a ramp to the dais and wheeling down on the other side. I was only too happy to oblige with a demonstration that I wouldn't need a pusher; the ramp wasn't quite as steep as the south col of Everest and, being me, I was determined to make it solo.

All the recipients were then gathered in a room, our names were called and we were sorted into groups according to our ranking and issued with little hooks which were fixed to our jackets so that medals could be hung on easily. The preparations had the efficiency of a military operation — or of long and regular practice. Then everyone tried to pay attention as the master of ceremonies rattled through the procedure, which probably sounded to most of us like this: "When your name is called the citation will be read — you will proceed forward — walk up the ramp stop turn left bow curtsey or salute to His Excellency — take two steps forward — His Excellency will present you with your decoration — you will bow curtsey or salute again — take two steps back turn to your right — take two steps stop turn left bow curtsey or salute to Lady Blundell — take two steps back — turn right and proceed in orderly fashion down the ramp to the side where you will be met by an aide who will show you to your seat — after you are all present you will join friends and relatives and proceed through to the reception room — where there will be a receiving line — where you will meet various other Government officials including the Prime Minister Mr Kirk."

We were lined up and the knighthoods led off, followed by the other orders in descending rank. As a BEM, I was well aware I had a fair amount of time to fill in. Many of the assembly were looking rather dazed by this time; the instructions had clearly gone in one ear and out the other because they'd been petrified from the start. I tried chatting with the people nearby and asked one naval type what he was there for. He looked rather shocked by the question and then replied awkwardly, "I really don't know."

There was great activity in the room behind us, so I investigated and found stewards industriously covering all available table surfaces with hors d'oeuvres and cocktail preparations. Jokingly, I said to one of them, "Reserve that space for me when I come back later." He took this quite seriously and asked what I'd like to drink.

"Plenty of brandy and plenty of ginger ale. I never drink anything else," I said. "And hot savouries."

I then had time to study the enormous space of Government House and appreciate how cold and uncomfortable it was in the vast hallway where we were waiting. I eased up the line and peered through the curtains, thinking it was a pity to miss what was going on entirely. The first thing that struck me was the silence and solemnity and muted tones as the names were called, the citations read and another victim beckoned, tapped on the shoulder or forcibly shoved forward into the arena. I thought that after the citation and presentation there would have been some applause or trumpets or something; but, no, just a hushed and pregnant silence.

One or two of the services fellows stood rooted to attention for at least an hour, looking neither right nor left, and I'm sure by the time they were called up for their gongs they must have been literally frozen to the spot. Some of the recipients who may have remembered all the moves obviously forgot them immediately they got out there and saw all the people sitting there staring at them. I could see Sir Denis, talking from the corner of his mouth, correcting their manoeuvres so they arrived at the right place in the right order.

One old dear turned to leave the way she had come in and even I could hear him as he hastily whispered to her go the other way. Some of the keener military types practically saluted and heel-clicked themselves off the dais. One in particular moved himself about a foot every time he snapped to attention.

My name was called and I rolled into action. I could see Sir Denis looking rather nervously at me, wondering whether I was going to make it up the ramp and we were both probably concerned that my travel bag, which I refused to part with, was going to fall from my lap. It was rather a steep ramp and I knew I couldn't let go the wheels to grab the bag or I'd shoot backwards again. But I'd thought it out very carefully and I was just making the last few inches and preparing a left wheel when he very helpfully moved forward. I had my head bent and didn't notice.

He held out a hand to help me, I made my fast left wheel — and ran onto his foot. In fact the front castor rammed his foot deep into several inches of quality carpet.

Being the brave man he is, Sir Denis said grimly through clenched teeth, "Got me that time, didn't you. Don't move."

I couldn't anyway — and neither could he. He reached round with some difficulty, took the medal from the cushion and hung it on my hook, still maintaining a calm and smiling countenance while I went on grinding his foot into the carpet.

It must have been even worse when I had to back off and turn to move towards Lady Blundell, because of the swivelling action of the front wheel, but I finally let him have his poor foot back.

Lady Blundell was charming. She was delighted, she said, because she had happy memories of the para team in London and Edinburgh.

Then it was all over and I hit the downward ramp at high speed, heading straight for the handsome ceiling-to-floor windows — and seeing in my mind the next day's headline of my headlong leap through them. Then an aide, watching my descent with a growing look of horror on his face, abruptly intercepted and guided me to a place of safety.

All this had happened in complete, respectful silence and

I'm sure no-one in the audience had any idea of the drama enacted before their very eyes.

I met an elderly recipient from Opotiki who actually envied my mode of travel. He was getting round on two sticks and found the whole presentation rather an ordeal.

One of the last called was a young man from Wellington who received the George Cross for his bravery in tackling an armed robber in the street and overpowering him. It was the moment for the first crowd reaction. Everyone leaned forward when his name was called and the citation read and this was the only time when there was any noise at all. As he came out, everyone was murmuring the same thing: "Isn't he small?"

I next held up the receiving line while Lady Blundell and I had a long gossip about London, Edinburgh and our respective daughters. Then back to the hall where it all began and I was immediately grabbed by an aide with a cardboard box, who whipped my medal off, removed the hook and put it in the box with the explanation that it would be used again next time.

On to the bunfight — and my steward had indeed reserved me a space. I was ushered to a table where several brandies were already lined up at attention for attention. I settled happily into these — apart from a break when we were all rushed off to pose for Press pictures — but eventually we had to get back into the Wellington gale.

We were back at the Campbells' house in Khandallah before I discovered to my horror that in the hustle and bustle I'd left my precious sheepskin and cushion from my chair on the steps of Government House when we loaded the chair into the car boot. I can't travel far in comfort without them — there's no flesh on my bones to protect me — so we got on the phone to Government House and eventually learnt that they'd been found and could be collected from the porter's lodge, whatever or wherever that was.

The Campbells had to go off to work, so Garth and I decided to spend the afternoon at the rock opera "Godspell". We were lucky to get very good seats and, after a drink in the pub across the road, we enjoyed the show immensely. We then took off into the gathering dark and still-howling gale to Government House to retrieve my belongings. Garth found his way back there somehow, jumped out at the front steps and began ringing bells and pounding the door of the darkened building. No-one answered, so we explored round the side and found another door to hammer on and some lights in windows which indicated not everyone had gone out.

From the depths even I, sitting in the car, could hear various bolts being drawn and locks unlocked, and eventually a young liveried footman appeared, looked down his nose at Garth as he explained his mission and said, "I am very sorry, we cannot be disturbed as Their Excellencies are about to dine." Then apparently to reinforce the point, he unexpectedly pulled a large fob watch from a waistcoat pocket and looked meaningfully at it. Garth explained the urgency of his call and was eventually redirected back to the door where we had started our assault.

This was similarly unlocked and unbolted at great length and, with solemn dignity, the sheepskin and cushion were returned to us. By this time I was almost helpless with laughter, seeing it all in dumb show from the comfort of the car while Garth battled his way about in the gale, at times being blown backwards. He seemed to take ten minutes to cover the last lap from the door to the car with the sheepskin and cushion desperately clutched to his wind-battered body.

Since we both felt in a rather jolly state after all this nonsense we decided to round off the evening by visiting Carmen's night club. Garth, interestingly, seemed to know exactly where it was and vanished up the steep stairs to see if it was possible to get me and my chair up there. Carmen, he told me later, was most obliging and provided him immediately with two gentlemen, both, oddly enough, wearing white mackintosh raincoats, to help him with the long lift up from the street. We were startled and amused to discover from Carmen that they were members of the vice squad.

It was a highly entertaining end to the night. I thoroughly enjoyed the show, whips, strips, nudes and audience, and Carmen and his/her staff were most polite and attentive and kept us supplied with very good coffee. Garth even enjoyed a form of bonus, a lapful of statuesque blonde stripper — although his only comment on this experience was that she felt distinctly clammy to the touch.

When it all ended with a rather startling performance by a stripper who began in a leather outfit and ended with a couch and a formidably large stockwhip, the vice squad boys were still obligingly on hand to get me back down to the street again. We wondered if they were on permanent duty there and to what lengths Carmen's girls would have to go before they began to take any action.

Chapter Nineteen

We appeal to you

IMMEDIATELY after the Wellington trip we began the appeal to raise funds for a trust to aid the rehabilitation and housing of paraplegics, particularly new ones. The New Zealand federation decided to make it a nation-wide once-only appeal in three phases — a house-to-house collection, a canvass of business houses and an appeal to organisations — with a target of $500,000.

I became heavily involved during the next three months with a steady stream of promotions up and down the country with the chairman of the appeal, "JB" Munro, who was then M.P. for Invercargill. JB was an extraordinary man with great drive, determination and enthusiasm. At the end of it all, despite the exhaustion and frustrations that I experienced, I was delighted when the first report on the appeal specially noted that JB and I were personally responsible for raising $19,000. The effort, which at times seemed just too much, hadn't been in vain.

For weeks on end I met and addressed various service organisations, schools, clubs, business executives, public meetings, got involved with press, radio and television interviews, was photographed and filmed, and rushed hither and thither. But it was all most educating and illuminating.

On one Wellington trip, I was invited to dinner at Bellamy's. JB took me on a conducted tour of the cramped and uncomfortable old Parliament Buildings, where I was fascinated by the endless comings and goings of people. Yet I couldn't help comparing the lush and plush offices of businessmen that I had seen with the tatty, confined quarters from which Parliamentarians were expected to run the business of the whole country.

I got a seat in the back benches to watch the house in session; Rob Muldoon chaffed me for being on the wrong side, Tom McGuigan spouted on about the Port hills in Christchurch or something, the Speaker wasn't in his chair and Rob seemed to be the only one who actually looked alive and taking notice — although at one stage young energetic Mike Moore leapt to his feet on a point of order before rushing off to meet his lady friend for dinner. Actually, a number of M.P.s I'd met before seemed to be glad of my appearance as a distraction in a particularly boring day and came wandering across to say hello. I found the whole thing ludicrous and couldn't understand how it could work. I saw Sid James in a comedy play that night and told JB next day that he had nothing on Parliament comedy.

From Wellington I was put on a plane for New Plymouth, where, I was told, I'd be met by a Laurie Petty, who was organising the appeal in Taranaki. I'd never heard of Laurie until then. Now, I'll never forget him. Laurie had been a charity promoter in Taranaki for years and had been called out of retirement at very short notice for this one. Everybody else had been studying the problem and thinking about it for about six months; Laurie, knowing nothing at all about paras, was given just two weeks. He did an amazing job that made some of the other areas look pretty half-baked.

Perhaps because I was in a wheelchair he thought I'd be tireless, because he'd lined up a massive jaunt for me through the province. I was taken to schools, whipped aboard a naval vessel that conveniently for Laurie, happened to be in port, to a theatre show that, conveniently for Laurie, happened to be entertaining kids in New Plymouth, to service club dinners and luncheons, to Stratford, Eltham, Hawera, Patea and back to New Plymouth — all in one day. I was endlessly talking and travelling as Laurie swept us onward through the depths of a chilly Taranaki winter. He was so endlessly sociable and enthusiastic, I could have screamed; but he did a wonderful job, and for that you can forgive anyone.

The kids I met were hilarious. They're not at all inhibited like adults when confronted with someone like me, and they ask questions frankly and freely. One little boy wanted to know how I slept. This stumped me for a bit until I realised he thought I spent all my time in the chair and actually slept there. So I explained that paraplegics slept in beds like everybody else. He looked a little unconvinced so I added, "It's easy for us. We just throw our legs into bed and jump in after them." This was what they wanted to hear. They roared with delight. Another was fascinated to learn how, when I threw the discus, I went round and round in circles like able-bodied throwers do. I explained to him that we couldn't do that because they locked our chairs down. We had to throw the discus the hard way.

Laurie even found time in his incredible schedule to introduce me to a local para, Jack Charteris, who had established a thriving sandal-making business in New Plymouth employing other disabled people and also ran a radio-telephone business for the city. He was taking an amazingly active and successful role in the community and was also doing a man-sized job for the establishment of the trust.

The appeal was helped along by the making of a special film for TV in advance of the house-to-house canvass. This spelled out very clearly the need for the trust, especially when it explained how simply anyone could become a paraplegic — from a football tackle to a car smash to a quiet fall down a step. One man in Invercargill actually became a para while he was romping with his children. He rolled over awkwardly on his neck and was instantly paralysed.

At the height of the promotion, old Lady Luck snarled at me again. I was unaware that to give me warmth on a cold day a hot water bottle had been placed on a car seat for me. I can't feel pain in my legs, and I'd been sitting on it for long enough to cause a huge burn area before I found out. My heart nearly stopped: I'd enough experience of this kind of thing to know it could take months to heal and I could be laid up all that time and unable to help the appeal as I wanted to.

Fortunately, although it covered most of the back of one thigh, the burn was largely superficial. I was able to continue, getting local help with the constant dressings and treatments and rarely failing to meet my obligations. I had to spend a week in Whakatane Hospital to clean the area with saline treatment and take Savlon baths twice a day. Then I found a nurse brave enough to pick off all the slough, assuring her all the time that I couldn't feel a thing — even if she could — and went off home with a pillowcase full of dressings and equipment to get me through the campaign. I found I could treat the leg myself by propping it up in a bent position and using a mirror while I applied the dressings.

Quite soon after I resumed my travels, I called a doctor in Auckland in to dress the burn, and he nearly had a fit when he saw it. He said I should not only be in hospital, I should be having skin grafts. I told him I didn't have the time for that — I had to get the appeal over and done with first. Auckland at that time was desperately short of helpers and I was busy day and night.

The collection finally came off in August and, to our sheer delight, we raised around $300,000, far better than we had expected.

The burn scar isn't so bad, if you don't look at it too often.

While the fund promotion was on, Mum was admitted to Tauranga Hospital for a general check on her condition, and she died rather suddenly and tragically in September following a swift deterioration of her heart and kidneys. It was doubly sad because she'd just had word that Liz was bringing her two children home for a three-month holiday that summer. I had the unenviable task of calling Liz in Canada and telling her that Mum had gone; I made it worse for her by being so emotional that she had to wring the facts out of me by question and answer to get an explanation of my incoherent state.

She arrived in New Zealand the following week to help with the huge and thankless task of cleaning out the family home and then helping me to prepare for the Commonwealth Games which were coming up in Dunedin early in 1974. It was wonderful having her with us, and I got on fine with her children and even looked after them for a while so she could get away for a sight-seeing trip. The time flew until the Commonwealth Games were on us.

The thirty-strong New Zealand team got together a few days before the opening, and we all stayed in marvellous accommodation at the University of Otago. But the weather, frankly, was awful, for the whole time the temperature was never much above 8°C. God, it was cold. Most of the other teams had been told they were coming to the tropics in the summer, so they just weren't equipped for these conditions. My friend Maggie from Scotland arrived shaking and blue. She hadn't brought a single sweater with her. I knew how she felt. When you cross half the world with limited spending money, you don't want to have to blow most of it on clothing — and that's what I'd had to do to counter the cold in England and Scotland four years earlier.

The warmth of Dunedin's welcome helped a little to make up for the wet, bleak conditions, but it was tough going. We Kiwis wanted to train hard, but when you're out on an archery line and get hit by a hailstorm which soaks you before you can pack up and get to shelter, it's not easy. Many members of the team suffered from muscle stiffness and the physios with the team became the most important members of the support crew.

Dunedin and the paras had a real love affair. Thousands turned out to watch us. Most popular were the wheelchair basketball (hundreds were turned away from every session) and the swimming (it was the first time the huge Moana pool overflowed with spectators). And the voluntary help we got was outstanding. I was wheeling back from a venue one night and climbing a rather steep hill when two Boy Scouts raced up and helped me to the top. I accepted their help thankfully, and as it was rather late in the day said, "Aren't you sick of pushing paras up this hill?"

"Oh, no," one of them said cheerfully, "you're only my fifty-sixth today. We consider it a great honour to be able to do this, and anyway," he added with a cheeky grin, "we get lots of badges."

I noticed then that he was literally covered with them. But it's only because of this kind of help that paraplegic games can be held at all. Don't ever think we don't appreciate what people do for us. In Dunedin the Boys Brigade manned all the lifts, and all kinds of volunteers staffed the dining rooms and accommodation blocks.

The Kiwis again notched up a good tally of wins. For us it was the year of the discus. I was able at long last to get the distance I wanted and the world record (16.58 m), Graham Condon won his event and, a week or two later at the able-bodied games in Christchurch, Robin Tait got his discus gold medal. My personal tally was four golds (the discus, a 5.43 m shot, a 12.20 m Commonwealth Games javelin record, and the pentathlon, in which, because it was a better day, I had a

12.74 m javelin and 5.82 m shot) and two silvers in archery and darchery — I could have struck gold there, too, if I'd known a little more about bows and arrows.

It was a fun games all around apart from the weather. The students' hostel had a wonderful conversation pit with sheepskin rugs and a huge log fire. It was probably thought the paras would never use it because it was sunk well below floor level, but on closing night it was ringed with empty chairs and everyone was down in the pit in a tangle of arms and legs. Some of us even spent the entire night there.

Kel and the kids were down for the Games, which all helped, and when they headed away home via Nelson, I teamed with two Canadians, two Kenyans and an Aussie who all wanted to see the games in Christchurch, while many of the others took off to Queenstown. We were able to stay at the St John of God Hospital in Halswell and attend the games every day, and most of our nights were spent mixing in the village with the athletes and officials. It was an unforgettable experience.

We followed the decathlon closely, and on the afternoon it finished we met the New Zealander Mene Mene and the others in the village. They were looking totally exhausted, but Mene Mene told us dolefully that they still had one event to go for which he was trying to organise transport and a venue, but was having difficulty because it was still early in the games.

"Eh?" I asked. "What on earth would this be?"

He grinned. "It's a drinking contest."

I was able to offer him the use of a van which had been kindly allocated to us, so we all ended up eventually at a venue quite some distance from the village to contest their last big event. Some contest. They were so tired that after one or two beers they were all ready for bed.

With the games over, I had a little trouble getting out of Christchurch because all north-bound transport was heavily booked. I hadn't really planned that far ahead when I decided to stay on there. However, all problems are surmountable . . . and if you don't believe me, read on.

Chapter Twenty

When Kiwis can't fly

APRIL 17 1974 dawned a bright and beautiful day, and it was still cheerful sunshine as I flew out of Whakatane heading for a function in Blenheim to raise funds for intellectually handicapped children. Many games gold medallists, including weightlifters and both able-bodied and para athletes, had been invited, and I was looking forward to meeting old friends. I flew into Taupo, with the lake sprawled out under a blue sky, and there was no hint that anything other than a pleasant weekend was under way.

But, as we flew on high and smoothly for Wellington, I began to realise something was wrong in the state of euphoria. We should be heading down for Rongotai, but we were circling while Wellington was still a long way off. Funny — until the captain announced that because of inclement weather with high winds at Wellington we were diverting to Palmerston North. Oh well, high winds in Wellington weren't all that unusual, I thought.

We landed at Milson airport at Palmerston North to find other diverted aircraft already gathered in a homeless huddle and people milling about in all directions not knowing what to do with themselves now. Then, although Wellington airport was closed, I and other passengers ticketed for Wellington and beyond were bundled in taxis destined for Wellington Airport. I shared with a woman heading for Masterton, and worried stiff how she was going to get there, and a man with an enormous musical instrument in a case which he had to carry in the cab with him.

I was wondering vaguely how I was going to get out of Wellington once I got into it, and my wondering increased as we neared Wellington and could see the chaos the "high winds" (it was a blasted gale by now) were causing there. Huge waves pounded along the coast, trees were coming down, and I imagined everyone in the city was battening hatches and hanging on. We stopped at the NAC air centre in the city long enough to taste the confusion that existed there, and then I was taken out to Rongotai which, not unnaturally, was still closed to all traffic.

The reception desk told me all flights in or out were cancelled and that onward-bound passengers were being taken to Wellington hotels for the weekend because the storm showed no signs of abating and the forecast remained grim.

I asked about some Auckland athletes who were supposed to have joined me in Wellington and was told they'd been and gone. They'd tried the ferry, but Cook Strait was closed to all shipping. I had already experienced being grounded in Wellington, and the prospect of going through that again engendered a feeling of desperation. There had to be a way of getting across the water without relying on the short leap from Wellington to Blenheim.

Consultation with the staff and airline schedules informed me that Palmerston North, where I'd already been, was still open and that there was a flight going to Christchurch. In fact one had been going out when I was there — it could have got me south in ample time to get back up the coast to Blenheim. I calculated that if I could get this later flight, I could still make Blenheim by road in time for the function, if not for anything else. Which would be better than kicking my heels (figuratively) in Wellington. The desk staff were close to frenzy trying to cope with the hordes of stranded, but I managed to get an ear and put my case to it. The owner of the ear looked at me with considerable surprise, but eventually agreed I could give it a go if that was what I wanted.

I wheeled out of there and hailed a taxi. Overhead and on the ground the weather remained terrible. It was early afternoon, but dark and menacing, and the gale raged on mindlessly. The woman driver who picked me up was happy to take me into Wellington, but not on to Palmerston North. "I had two flat tyres last night and I don't really want to go out of town. I'll call you another cab."

So in Cuba Street she flagged down another cab. This driver agreed he could take me to Palmerston North, but he didn't have enough petrol aboard. Since we were then in the middle of the oil crisis and petrol was being rationed, we had a new problem. He also looked as if he'd been up all night and he didn't speak very good English, but I was still looking for action.

I got it. In the middle of my transferring to his cab, the gale whipped my wheelchair off in one direction and sent the sheepskin sailing away in another. The drivers hared off after them, captured them, brought them back and then the wind whipped the bonnet of the taxi up with a force that nearly tore it off its hinges.

Eventually we got on the road to Palmerston North. The driver was going at a maddeningly slow pace for someone with a plane to catch. He explained haltingly that he was going to stay well below the limit because he'd got some speeding tickets the day before and he was terrified of the consequences of getting another one.

About 3 p.m., as we were nearing Palmerston North, he added a fresh complication by asking me where the airport was. I've been round a bit, but Palmerston North is one of the places I haven't been around a bit in, so I hadn't the faintest idea. So he had to stop several times to ask people for directions because his poor English only seemed to result in worse confusion. Perhaps, as always seems to happen, everyone he asked was equally a stranger. After the fifth attempt, some kind of message got through and we finally came within sight of the airport. I could see a plane coming in and I decided immediately that was the one I should be on. My heart sank because there is no such thing as a para in a hurry — and there's no way a para can make a frantic last-minute dash up an aircraft gangway while the pilot revs the engines. Everything has to be moved according to a system or nothing moves at all.

But luck was with me. There was time before take-off, even for a para, and I was finally loaded into the Christchurch-bound flight. There was no shortage of planes at Milson; they were all over the place huddling from the storm — but it wasn't the National Airways network that took us out of there, it was little old Mt Cook Airlines. And despite all the people I'd seen in Wellington who were frantically trying to get south, there were only ten of us aboard.

One of them was Gladys Donaldson, who was also heading for Blenheim and had figured out the same route as I had.

She was equally puzzled why the airline hadn't scheduled more passengers onto it instead of heaping them all up in pubs in Wellington. It seemed inexplicable that with all these people trying to get south, aircraft should be stranded empty at Palmerston North while another airline made the only flight across the storm.

We reached Christchurch after 5 p.m. and calculated that if we could get a cab we could still make Blenheim in time for the dinner. I got NAC to ring the function organisers and tell them I was on the way because I realised that by now, having heard nothing of me and plenty of the disruption to transport, they'd have given up hope of any of the North Island guests getting through.

So Gladys and I got into cab number four — and very quickly got out again when a passerby pointed out to the genial driver that we had a flat rear tyre. He was more than willing to take us north but he didn't have a reliable spare and couldn't get one from his depot. So, with valuable time trickling away, he called up taxi number five.

This was driven by enthusiastic David Woods, who smartly got into the action but first had to make a wide detour to fill up with that precious petrol at a special depot. I was roundly cursing the Arabs by this time, and beginning to realise I was going to be late. It was all becoming pointless, but since we'd got this far we decided we might as well press on. Going back on our tracks seemed to have even less point. Gladys, an English girl with a fine wit and sharp turn of phrase, joined in whole-heartedly and we had a lot of laughs as we finally headed north. As she would say quaintly, "And why not indeed?"

The Kaikoura coast was wild. The sea was smashing in across the rocks onto the road, there were numerous rock-falls and our rapid progress was abruptly stopped when David swung round a corner and went straight over a large boulder smack in the middle of the highway. It was startling to see the steering wheel almost come adrift in his hands as the steering box was ripped out of the bottom of the car. By a miracle, we missed several power poles and came to rest a short distance from the pounding surf by the road edge. We were shaken but unhurt. David will probably never forgive us, but all Gladys and I could do was look at each other and collapse in helpless laughter. The whole expedition had become totally ludicrous.

Traffic was thin on that lonely stretch of road on that foul night, but eventually a car appeared and gave David a lift back to a house so he could phone ahead to Kaikoura for a replacement taxi and back to Christchurch for a tow truck to come and drag him away. Many power and phone lines were down, so this took time. Rather than leave us sitting there alone, David made his way back to us and we all huddled together trying to console each other and keep warm. If we hadn't kept laughing I think we would have cried. It seemed ages before the Kaikoura taxi pulled up and took us aboard, leaving David behind to wait for his tow.

Taxi number six got us there — although I was no longer in time for the function. But one of the organisers had stayed up — some mysterious grapevine had kept them informed that I was slowly but steadily approaching. I almost fell from the cab in relief and collapsed again when he asked cheerily, "What kept you?" The time — 2 o'clock in the morning.

Because of taxi etiquette, taxi number six was then obliged to call out a Blenheim cab to take Gladys her last few kilometres to Woodbourne — so that made it seven for the trip. I went straight to bed and to sleep, but I breakfasted with the people who ran the function and heard what a tremendous success it had been anyway. I spent the day with the I.H.C people and was able to amuse them with my saga. But one little boy said to his mother afterwards, "Mrs Rimmer makes up good stories, doesn't she?"

What I didn t know was that a local reporter had taken it all down and wired it all over New Zealand. So everyone joined in the laughs. Back home a week later, I got a letter from David Woods. He'd read the press report and thought I'd be interested in the hitherto unpublished sequel. He'd stayed until the truck arrived, with rocks still tumbling down around him and waves breaking right across the car at times and threatening to sweep him away. He'd finally got back to Christchurch at 10 a.m. But the Kaikoura taxi, going home after delivering Gladys and me, suffered the same fate as his, hitting a rock and wrecking itself.

David said he thought I'd like to know about the trail of destruction I'd left behind me. Checking back, I realised I'd involved two aircraft, seven cabs, two crashes, some flat tyres, a runaway wheelchair, a tow truck or two and had only been prevented from keeping my engagement by a bloody rock I'd never even met. I was, in fact, the only North Islander who made it to Blenheim.

That must prove something — but the only thing I can think of is that I'm pig-headed.

With Liz back in Canada and Mum no longer there, Edgecumbe wasn't the same any more and we decided it was time for a change. Kel was travelling thirty-two kilometres a day between Edgecumbe and Whakatane and, since he was quite happy with his job there with the radio station, we reasoned it was time we shifted home into Whakatane. Since we didn't want to load ourselves with another mortgage by building a new home, we looked around for an older house we could adapt. We realised that anything we found would have to be changed for a wheelchair, but we finally found a rather large house in Douglas Street, very handy to the centre of town, the schools and all the other facilities. We moved in in June 1974.

About the same time Ailsa got the same urge, and she and Rhys left Tauranga and moved south into a house only a few doors along the street. So we were suddenly both re-united with Ian and we filled the local schools and activities with a rush of Davies cousins — eight of them.

We found it was certainly different living in an older house, but since we were used to it we quite happily got stuck into the fairly major structural alterations we needed. Access was the main problem, of course. This architectural barrier pops up everywhere. There was no garage, so we combined a front-door carport with a ramp which eliminated the steps. We built another ramp to the back door. The inevitable hand-basin and storage went in alongside my bed. We beat the laundry problem by buying an automatic washer and drier, although I can now wheel quite easily to the rotary line and load and unload it from the chair when the weather's OK.

I spent hours on my backside outside, trying to create order out of the chaos. The place was a mass of weeds and overgrowth, and it was great exercise and training to spend a few hours tearing it out with my bare hands. The bigger stuff I sawed up to feed the fire, which again should have helped to build bigger and bonnier throwing muscles. The major assault was reserved, partly for financial reasons, for the bathroom. Getting into the bathroom, let alone the bath, was like tackling an obstacle course because the door opened inwards towards the bath and handbasin and I had to back and fill and swear steadily to manoeuvre my chair in so that I could do what I had to do without being wide open to everyone using the hall.

But the general spaciousness of the place, particularly in the kitchen, was a joy once I'd learnt that to prepare meals was going to involve a lot more travelling than I was used to in Edgecumbe house. You can't just reach around and grab things in a kitchen about 3.66 m wide and 6.1 m long. When we moved in the stove was jammed right in a corner; that had to come out into the middle of the long wall. I sometimes wonder how people ever managed to plan homes as crazily as that.

September was a thrill. JB Munro contacted me about a forthcoming visit by Raymond Burr, the wheelchair detective in TV's "Ironsides", who was finally coming out at the invitation of Norman Kirk. He was attending a dinner in Auckland the first night and a luncheon in Wellington the following day in support of Auckland's Laura Ferguson Trust for the Disabled and the Paraplegic Trust. I was invited to spend the day in Wellington with him. I'd already promised to talk in Gisborne that night for the Crippled Children Society, but the obvious transport problem was quickly and speedily overcome. The Ministry of Transport turned on its beautifully equipped Fokker Friendship, complete with lounge bar, to fly Raymond to Whakatane, gather me up and then drop me in Gisborne on the way back from Wellington later in the day.

It was a great day for Whakatane. Hundreds turned up at

the airport to greet Ironsides, who turned out to be a genial
giant of a man, enormous in stature, generous in nature and a
real delight to be with. He was suffering from travel exhaustion and I could sympathise with him, but he was still untiring
in his geniality and generosity. The only time I saw him sit
down and relax was on the aircraft.

The whole day was a great success. We met Bill Rowling,
by now Prime Minister, had an interview on Radio Windy,
and met a chap named Phil Harkness, who was then working
with Raymond on the establishment of a newspaper in Fiji.
By the time I left him I was ready to chuck everything and
join the Ironsides gang — just to go on enjoying the pleasure
of his company. He was heading back to Auckland for a
dinner that night with film magnate Sir Robert Kerridge, so I
suggested he should mention to Sir Robert the inaccessibility
to paraplegics of so many of his chain of theatres, including
the one in Whakatane.

The crowd that greeted him at Gisborne had to be seen to
be believed. People had come from all around for the chance
of a glimpse of him, so it was a huge bonus for the organisers
of the dinner at which I was speaking for some of the crippled
children to be there to meet the great man. Although it was
an additional demand on him, he was unfailing in the way he
spread his friendliness over them all. It was a wrench to think
that I'd probably never see him again — he made that kind of
impression on people. But I had to pull myself together and
get on with my own job.

A team of disabled athletes including a few paraplegics
went off to the first Fespic (Far East and South Pacific)
Games in 1975 but I was quite happy not to be a contender
for the team but to stay at home and prepare for the
Olympics in Canada. In any case, members of the team were
allowed to enter only one field or track event and one swimming event and there was no pentathlon. It was, in fact, a
good trip for athletes who hadn't been to other international
events.

The Toronto Olympics were also covering blind and
amputee athletes for the first time, requiring up to 40 cate-

gories for every event on the programme. New Zealand was planning a team of only 12 so I had to concentrate hard on my weaker pentathlon events, swimming and archery. I cancelled all my social engagements and immersed myself totally in hours of training. All speaking engagements — and there were many invitations — were out. Every morning, and it was moving in to winter, saw me at the local hot springs where sometimes the steam was so dense it was like swimming in fog.

I took part in all the local archery club shoots and had a backyard target to work with. With the help of various expert archers around the country, I improved my scoring almost 100 per cent.

Then, one morning in March, the phone rang beside my bed, I picked it up and a voice said: "You're in, old girl." It was Jim Savage.

"Gee, thanks, Jim," I said, then, and it was an awkward pause, " . . . and you?"

'Oh, yeah, they're taking us oldies," said Jim cheerfully. "But we'll have to work. It's going to be tough over there."

I grabbed a pen and wrote a fast letter to Liz telling her I was coming and that we were an experienced team. There were six of us from Israel and all the other six had represented New Zealand at one meeting or another since then. Unexpectedly, no other disabled athletes were chosen, which was a pity. And, once again, I was the only woman.

We assembled in Auckland on 30 July with the cloud of the black boycott at the Montreal Games uppermost in our minds. We were all wondering what, if any, effect it would have on us in Toronto. We knew a multi-racial South African team would be there, but we fervently hoped the meeting would continue without any political interference.

Getting myself organised away for this trip had had an extra complication because while I would be in Canada, Julie would be off to Australia with 30 other Whakatane High pupils for a netball and volleyball tour. I'd been involved in the family and school fund-raising efforts; I couldn't really avoid them because as well as being a parent I was also a pupil, having joined night classes in University Entrance English and School Certificate German that year.

This was the class Jane & I attended
—Eileen

I went off to Canada just a bit miserably because I had hoped to stay in Toronto with Liz and her family but the team management wouldn't allow it. As it turned out, Liz practically joined the team anyway. And many of us arrived in Canada even more miserably, because we were ill with a strange virus which we apparently carried with us from New Zealand. We had hot, dry, sore eyes, high temperatures, sore throats, and some of us were affected right through the games. It didn't help that the weather was erratic and unseasonal and we were out in rainy and cold conditions for hours on end during some of the field events. Every one of my events, in fact, was held in bad weather. The virus also got some of our escorts. I thought I had escaped it, but it caught me when we reached Toronto and stayed with me for the first few days of the games.

So we were a tired, bedraggled, red-eyed bunch when we straggled into York University, where most of the paraplegics were accommodated, at 1.30 a.m. and then endured several hours of medical gradings, documentation, security screening, official photography and so on before getting to bed. Liz found me during all this and I discovered that she had been detailed as a volunteer worker in the medal presentation area.

The Toronto accommodation was superb, but with the huge number of differing events catering for the various grades of paras as well as the blind and the limbless, the organisation was a little less so. The days were long and exhausting for all of us; we had to get up early to beat the queues for the bathrooms and the lifts. I found one of the boy scouts on lift duty crying quietly in a corner one day. He'd lost the manual key, so the lift was stopping at every floor and he was being sworn at in every language in the world for the time each trip was taking.

Then we had to queue for the dining room and for the buses to the stadium some 45 to 60 minutes drive away. My first event didn't get under way until late afternoon and it was still in its final stages at 10 p.m., because the competition was tough, especially from my old Austrian and German rivals from Israel and Munich. I had time to practise my night-school German; I think the only mistake I made was to ask them in best textbook tones how many children they had. Since none of them was married, it wasn't entirely tactful and the replies were very firmly negative.

I led the qualifiers with 13.98 m and as it was getting colder and wetter by the minute the coach and I decided not to take my last three throws. There was no hope of breaking a world record and no one else got past my qualifying mark. So I finally got my first gold medal at 11.30 p.m. and, to my delight and astonishment, Liz not only organised the presentation but was there to give me my medal. The few remaining New Zealand supporters, Liz and I and the tall black chief organiser all burst into tears in the emotion of the moment. It was an unforgettable beginning to the games.

I suffered from our friendly virus for the next two days, but I managed to win the shot and score well in my pentathlon events and then finally reached the javelin final at the end of a tiring day. I was feeling far from enthusiastic but added more golds to my collection by winning both.

The darchery event was held on the last day and in preparation for it Bill Lean, Graham Garrett and I rested up at the university. At 11 a.m., a security guard raced up the stairs, found us and told us the event had started an hour ago. The times had been changed but no one had told us and I was still in bed. Something, somewhere, went wrong with the computer.

I can't attempt to describe exactly what it feels like to be told you are an hour late for an event when you know it is going to take at least an hour to get to it anyway. And when you know it is an event which calls for calm, collected concentration, not a puffing, perspiring, last-second late arrival.

Our coach was still arguing with the officials when we arrived and discovered we were the only country which had not been told of the time change. Anyway, coach Ian Brown argued well and we were allowed to compete, even though the 60 m end had already been fired. We were told we could shoot that afterwards and that the inevitable protests would be over-ruled. We didn't have time for any sighting shots, so we started badly, but we slowly pulled ourselves together. I even got a perfect 10 with one arrow, but that was wiped out because I'd fired too soon. I was still staggered to find myself second over-all in the women's event. Protests were lodged and thrown out but, the following day, when the medals were to be presented, we learnt another last-minute protest had gone in and only the gold medal would be awarded. I haven't heard yet what happened to the silver and bronze medals or the protest.

As a team, we did well. Dennis Miller of Rotorua set world records in his track and slalom events, Bill Lean of Dunedin, even with flu, broke the world shot put record, Jim Savage got a bronze in the shot, Paul Chambers (Napier) a bronze in swimming and Reuben Ngata, Fred Creba, Brian McNicholl (Christchurch) and Ross Hines (Tauranga) were all medal winners, to give us a total of 14.

Our fears of boycotts were not unfounded, unfortunately, although New Zealand was not accused of anything in the way it was in Montreal. Instead, the hate was turned on South Africa; many teams refused or were not allowed to compete and the Poles and some other teams pulled out altogether. Jamaica, one of the most popular teams, was the first to withdraw.

The only comment I have made is that it was primarily the athletes who suffered.

I was able to see some of the blind and disabled events; and it was one of the highlights of the games to see a young fit Canadian with one leg high jump 1.86 m. And another to watch blind athletes run a 100 m sprint record only one second slower than the world record.

I saw Liz almost every day but was only able to get away to her home for one hour-long visit, such were the stress-filled conditions under which we operated for the whole stay. We were both physically and emotionally drained when we finally said goodbye. We headed for home with a brief stop at Los Angeles (in which the boys tried to see the whole of Disneyland from the wheelchairs in two hours) and a glorious three-day rest in Honolulu — the most beautiful and relaxing time of my life.

I rather upset my homecoming welcome. We reached Auckland ahead of schedule and I got an earlier plane than planned, to Whakatane, which really upset the airport reception organisation.

My most treasured prize from Canada was a magnificent

new bow and I began shooting it in immediately because I had my eye on the New Zealand able-bodied championship in Tauranga in September. This was a new experience and a complicated one because, with the rest of them, I had to shoot three arrows at a time and move on and off the line instead of staying right through. But I was delighted to win a trophy for the women's C-grade competition. Archery is one of the few sports in which the paraplegic and the able-bodied can compete on equal terms. Right now it is a sport that appeals to me just as much as the competitions organised specifically for the disabled, because it greatly enlarges the element of involvement which is so vital to all paras.

Chapter Twenty-one

Speaking of people

I'LL NEVER forget the first time I was invited to speak on my experiences. It was after my first overseas trip. I'd been carrying on endlessly for about two hours when I suddenly realised that, although I was supposed to be telling them about Israel, I still hadn't got past Singapore on the way over. There were so many incidents that I thought were relevant that, possibly, it would have taken me until the next day to finish. Still, if my audience was beginning to wonder if I was ever going to get to the point, they politely didn't show it.

This is probably a trap of ad lib speaking, but unless I want to remind myself of points I specifically intend to make, I don't use notes. I've tried to develop the technique of talking according to my audience and the reactions I get from them. I like to establish the feeling that I'm talking personally, and referring to notes spoils that spontaneity.

And after all the speeches I've made — in 1974 I was away from home fifty times on speaking trips, some of them involving several engagements — I'm still keyed up, nervous, sweating profusely (and it's nothing to do with the heat) before I begin. I think everyone who goes before an audience must be nervous. It's rather like competing in a sports event. The worst thing is that I can never eat much beforehand, which is a tragedy when I'm speaking at a bountiful sit-down dinner and have to pick away at my food while everyone else wolfs into the goodies.

But once I cleared the hurdle of that first speech, I went ahead accepting every invitation I could. I felt I was helping all paraplegics by travelling the country trying to make other people understand what we are all about. It's understanding we want, not sympathy. Paras are normal people who can play a normal part in life; if I've got just that message across to just some people, I've contributed something. Very often I've encountered people barriers as insurmountable as architectural ones.

The invitations to be a guest speaker multiplied fairly rapidly — the more I talked the more I was asked to talk. I guess I was novelty value to some extent, but also I believe more and more people were beginning to see us as a group who needed help and could be helped. So once I got over the initial difficulties, I was pleased to have the chance to promote the para movement (and delighted by the many useful contributions which came in for paraplegic association finances).

Of course whenever I got the chance I had a slam at architectural barriers, because I knew from experience that almost no able-bodied people even thought about them. Little things — like public phones you can't use because you can't get through the phone box door or reach the phone from outside because it's too high. Speaking in New Plymouth, I made a point of this because I'd discovered that New Plymouth's smart new airport didn't have a telephone we could use. I was invited back later to become the first para to use the one they installed for us. It was a satisfying little triumph.

I was once asked to speak at a subscription dinner in Porirua to raise funds for a community recreation centre. I went because I thought it was a worthwhile gesture, and during the function I raised the question of architectural barriers with the organisers. Were any involved in the design of the centre? They said they didn't know until they looked at the plans. Later I was told that they did find them and called a special meeting to change the plans before it was too late.

More and more designers are making allowances for disabled people these days, I'm happy to say. New buildings have wider doors, ramps, easier access and so on. But even so, the stone walls and barricades confront us constantly and block our efforts to be as independent of help as we want to be. As we must be. A minor thing — like a footpath kerb that's too high to cross unaided — is a major frustration. A public toilet that you can't get into is even worse. It may be easy enough to ignore or forget these matters — unless people are reminded that there are, in fact, thousands of us who are entitled to be remembered.

I found that getting through to people en masse wasn't as

difficult as I anticipated. If I believed in what I was talking
about — and I did — it wasn't difficult for me to talk.

I experienced real hostility only once. I was addressing a
meeting in a Taranaki rural area. I could sense that many of
the audience thought I was overstating the problems of paras
in New Zealand, that they were regarding me as a bludger on
their good natures and, perhaps worse, their bank accounts.
Sure, I admit I exaggerate at times, to make a point or to
heighten interest, but I don't embroider by telling lies. The
attitude at this meeting got under my skin; I was tired and at
the end of a long week of lectures and meetings.

Finally, I said angrily: "OK, so you don't believe the
problem exists. But if your son broke his neck diving into a
stream or in a motor-cycle accident or on a rugby field and
was a paraplegic for the rest of his life, I bet you'd believe it
then." I think — I hope — I got through to them.

Going away from home overnight or for weekends wasn't
too difficult. I drove myself if the meetings were within
reasonable distance and I always got back home the same
night if I could. But for the longer trips Mum was a wonderful
standby, always willing to be with the kids. Kel, anyway, is a
real home body. He has his garden and his workshop and he'd
rather be at home than anywhere else. I once got him to join
the Jaycees, but he wasn't really interested. So there was no
question of a deserted home and neglected kids while mother
kicked up her heels around New Zealand.

But it did make life damned busy, because I wasn't going
to let the demands on my time interfere with our family life
completely, and the kids had a multitude of activities like
athletics, swimming and gymnasium. There were also school
meetings, holiday outings, camping and other things we did
together that I prized highly. And I was determined to carry
on running a smooth household and keep up my own training
and conditioning programme. It wasn't a question of making
room for speaking engagements by dropping something else;
they had to be fitted into the existing schedule.

Maybe it was all part of that subconscious need that I
mentioned earlier to prove myself in the eyes of others.
Whatever it was, it was busy and it was tiring and it added
new frustrations. Any activity means frustrations for paras.

The mere act of getting up in the morning requires a major mental effort because it's so involved and takes so much time. We can't spring up and do things the simple way. We call it paraplegic time. It's even required for such mundane tasks as putting shoes on. Imagine yourself preparing a meal, doing every movement of the normal person — from a wheelchair. You can't just carry an item from one place to another because you need your hands to back, turn and propel yourself.

You get up in the morning, slip into slippers and dressing gown, stroll to the kitchen, fill the jug, plug it in and make an early morning drink. You don't even think about what you're doing. I can't do that. Before I get up I've got to detach and replace my overnight drainage, shower, dress while I'm sitting down, hoist myself into my chair, wheel through at least two doorways, back and fill and turn between the tap and the hotpoint with the jug, back and turn and fill between the table and the cupboards and the refrigerator for the tea things. And if I'm out of milk, I don't just nip out to the gate for a new bottle. That's a small example of paraplegic time.

I present, I'm told, a happy outgoing face. It's a defence mechanism. I smile (up to four hours non-stop at public functions) because if people see a para who isn't smiling they assume something is wrong. I am expected to smile and be happy in front of people who obviously don't feel they have to bother to make the same effort themselves. Another para, known for his happy outward nature and endless bounce, once told me he etched his grin on his face because he couldn't stand people asking him what was wrong every time they saw him without a smile; so I'm not just speaking from my own experience.

It has been suggested to me that perhaps, in retrospect, my accident wasn't such a disaster. I've been around the world more than once. I am well-known and in demand. I get around and meet people. I'm constantly active. I've been given a medal by the Government and a whole bunch more by the Olympic and Commonwealth paraplegic movements. I've flown up and down New Zealand like a tennis ball with Cook Strait as the net. I've luxuriated in the best hotels and motels and wined and dined from here to there and back again.

I guess it seems marvellous to be able to travel the way I do, but for paras travelling isn't fun. It's tiring, frustrating, tedious, a fundamental pain. I've spent hours, probably totalling whole days of my life, trapped in airports waiting for flight connections. If it's in Auckland, for instance, I can't, like everybody else, dash off for a cup of coffee to fill the time because the damned cafeteria's up a flight of stairs. How's that for an architectural barrier? There is at times no barrier bigger than the one between me and the coffee pot at Auckland International Airport.

And the talk tours have cost me a lot of money, particularly in the early days. It didn't seem to occur to a lot of people who asked me to speak for them to wonder about my expenses. I raised a lot of money, for para clubs, the movement as a whole and the para trust, but the donations I got very often didn't include anything for my travel and accommodation costs. Fortunately, it's a different scene now — and I'm making sure of it.

I've caused resentment in my time. There was a furore some time ago on remarks I made about the mounting football injuries — at the time the spinal unit in Christchurch had just taken in three boys with broken necks, there was another in Rotorua and a fifth in Dunedin. It made me realise that people don't want to be told unpleasant truths, and they don't want to be challenged to become involved. I'm all right and harmless if I entertain them with witty anecdotes, but they bridle if I start pricking their consciences with some of the harder facts of life.

I've even stirred some anti feeling in my own movement. Some of my greatest critics are the very people I, in my way, am trying to help.

I remember what Rob Muldoon told me on criticism and how to handle it. He said: if you believe sufficiently in a cause then you must go ahead regardless of criticism and do what you believe in. You can't allow yourself to be turned off by people who don't understand what you are trying to do and why you are trying to do it, and who would not do it themselves.

Because I've been active all round the country and fairly

frequently in the public eye, perhaps because I specialise in field events in sport, because I've trained myself to be forthright and aggressive in most situations, I've been called tough and hard. It's even been suggested that I'm not feminine. Well, maybe I'm not feminine — but I am a woman, with a woman's instincts and desires. Nothing has taken those away from me. Probably if I was a feminine woman, I would not have succeeded in sport. But I have all the feelings and emotions of a woman all right.

Because you've never seen me cry, it doesn't mean I don't.

I'll say this for Rob Muldoon. He recognised this the first time we met and the second time paid me the greatest compliment he could. He stood up and told an audience we were both addressing, "This Eve girl is all woman." I could have kissed him.

Most people don't know the real me — the me who lets go in private but never in public. I have deep depressions when I am alone — largely because of frustration. I don't envy other people, but I do regret for myself that there are so many things that are denied me despite the apparent freedom and rewards I've enjoyed.

I would swap them all, everything I've had out of life, for two ordinary legs that work. ·

To get up and dance again.

To run down a beach and plunge into the sea.

To ride a bike through the countryside.

To walk free with the wind in my face.

To feel the grass between my toes.

OTHER BOOKS FROM REEDS

Most Happy Fella by Beryl Te Wiata. The biography of the late Maori singer Inia Te Wiata, written by his wife — from his childhood in Otaki to stardom at Covent Garden and the Met.

Tooth and Nail by Mary Findlay. The powerful story of a young New Zealand girl in the depression days of the thrities. She describes a variety of jobs and conditions in stark, real terms.

Amiria by Anne Salmond. The story of Amiria Manutahi Stirling, a revered Auckland Maori elder who celebrated her 80th birthday in 1976. The unique story of her life, including an arranged marriage in 1918.

Thinking Dolphins, Talking Whales by Frank Robson. New Zealander Robson is an expert on the behaviour of dolphins and whales. He has exciting theories about many aspects of their behaviour, including non-verbal communications between man and dolphins.